# In
# Bed
# with
# a
nake

## from Defilement to Deliverance
## of Sexual Demons

Disclaimer:
Real names have been changed
to protect the identities
of those involved.

# In
# Bed
# with
# a

nake

My Predestined Testimony

Linda D. Lee

Foreword by Bishop Jeffery D. Thomas, Sr.

*"Where we listen to the Clouds"*

ISBN: 978-0-9979068-0-6

Printed on Acid Free Paper.

*Father,*

*In the name of Jesus
and by the power
of the Holy Spirit*

*Thank you for using
my infirmities to assist someone
in reaching their eternity.*

*I pray this book
glorifies your holy and divine name
Amen.*

# *Acknowledgements*

**To my immediate family**: Joe and Nelline Bridgewater, James and Roberta Duffey, Kenny and Darlene Goldsby and JoAnn Bridgewater; **Spiritual sisters and brothers**: Sis. Jacqueline Johnson, Sis. Sherrie Bradden, Sis. Shannon Collins, Sis. LaTonya Dacus, Sis. Tonya Williams, Rev. Terrell Collins and John (Jai) Freeman; **Spiritual leader and mentors**: Bishop Jeffery D. Thomas Sr. (thanks for giving to me so freely), Pastor Roy Elton Brackins and First Lady Pamela Brackins, Pastor Patrick Diggs, Evangelist Elaine/Kendra Mayes, I love and appreciate your teaching and wisdom. Thanks for your prayers, knowledge and understanding during this season. May God bless you a hundredfold. To Sis. Mary Rhodes, Rev. John Hendrix, and Kris Craig, thanks for your collective prayers and encouraging words while embracing my assignment. You have given birth to a new elevation of wisdom that you share without hesitation. To Rev. Lafayette Kelly and Rev. Christopher Smith, I thank the Holy Spirit for allowing you to birth: "We are positioned for a purpose", "Our success is based on our faith", "The devil wants what is birth inside of us. He wants you to have a spiritual abortion", Luke 24: 36-43, and "Our life should be a direct reflection of our saltiness for our children to see"… Mat 5: 13. To Prophetess

Ketra Wilkerson, bless the prophetic warning to remove some things from my life that could kill me. To Sis. Gail Smith, thanks for your perseverance in contacting me at work. I received the prophetic word from the Holy Spirit to finish my assignments because the Lord is waiting to bless the desires of my heart. To Secret Fire, thanks for your confronting and challenging attitude that forced me to acknowledge my suppressed issues. The Lord perfectly positioned you and our June 2006 break-up. It was time for me to correctly heal and walk into my purpose and assignment. **Last but not least:** To my son, Martell Perry, over the years I tried to provide a better life for you. I don't believe you truly understood the pressure I was under as a single mother raising a young man. I thank God for his sustaining power and hedge of protection He placed around us. I hope you read this book with an open mind while trying to understand who I was verses who God called me to be, a Woman of God. Initially, there were things about my past that I didn't discuss with you for a reason. However, now is my season to discuss all those things to try and help, not just you, but many others in a similar situation. It is my desire that after you read this book you will assist me in breaking our family's generational curse and lustful strongholds. I love you and will always be here for you. But, the best friend you will EVER have is the Lord. Learn to lean and depend only on him. Love, Mom

# Table of Contents

Prayer .................................................................v

Acknowledgement ...........................................vii

Foreword ..........................................................xi

### Part One
### Defilement to Deliverance

1   Introduction: My Soul Cried ...........................1

2   You Can Run But You Can't Hide ..................11

3   From Devastation… .......................................19

4   To God's Revelation .....................................49

### Part Two
### Back 2 Basics

5   "Virtuous" Defined ......................................71

6   Traits of a Godly Man — Before He Sinned .............77

7   Healing Beyond the Past ..............................81

8   Internal Healing and Deliverance .................85

## Part Three
## Advice Guide

9    The End Result....................................................93

10   Who's Touching Your Children?...........................99

11   How to be Comfortable In Your Singleness..............109
      Sistah to Sistah................................................113
      Games We Play ..............................................116
      Man Up! ........................................................124

12   Relationship Wisdom.......................................129

13   A Hot Mess! ...................................................139

*Foreword*

The candidacy of Sis. Johnson's book *In Bed with a Snake* resounds the word of God where Paul says, *"strong meat is for those who are full age."* Hebrews 5:14. I would like to admonish those who view this material as the <u>real</u> reality of the war going on today. It's written, *"For we wrestle not against flesh and blood, but against principalities, against powers, against the rulers of the darkness of this world, against spiritual wickedness in high places."* Ephesians 6:12 NKJV.

It appears that the canvas of our time has been painted with the paint of perversion and framed by the inability to endure sound doctrine. We have allowed demonic possession to navigate our circumstances. Demonic possession means to be driven by something that operates and controls you. Random House Webster's Dictionary.

.................

"Some folks have uncultivated regions in their life. There are areas that have been uninhabited by human beings. Some of you have some dolls. Some of you have toys; inanimate objects that have no life. They were used to cultivate your life. So you look for real love based on a battery operated orientation. Because a human cannot make you feel like an inanimate object has...I have been in the wild. Runaway child, running wild! I have been footloose and fancy free. I have been in places where anything goes. No rules, no legislature, no regulations. I have been in the wild. If you learn how to let the spirit lead you, God knows how to cultivate you."

Excerpt from sermon: 'Driven by the Spirit'
Bishop Jeffery D. Thomas, Sr.

...................

In Mark 1:12, the Holy Spirit immediately drove Jesus into the wilderness. God had to get Jesus ready in the wild so he could handle what was called civilization. A wilderness experience shows you what is inside of you. *In Bed with a Snake* deals with the author's own wilderness experience in dealing with sexual immorality. She was in the wild being cultivated for such a time as this. Please keep in mind, God will have you spend time by yourself so you will know how to handle people when you resurface from the wilderness.

But, there are times when God is not leading us; he is pressuring us into our purpose. And that is actually what happened to this Woman of God. Since the day I met Linda Johnson, she has done things as God wants things done... decent and in order. Upon uniting with the Mount Rose Church she has experienced an open, honest and explosive expression of her relationship with Jesus Christ. I personally believe she is a gift to the Body of Christ and a warrior in the master's campaign against Satan and sin. There is a message the Father gave to me to address with the people of God. It reminds me of the attitude of Linda, entitled, "A Good Soldier" where Paul instructs Timothy to endure hardness as a good solider. It's my earnest desire that the readers of *In Bed with a Snake* be able to comprehend the breath, length, depth and height of the compassion God has for us. Also, understand the strength of your spirit in the deliverance from strongholds and dominations in your life.

....................

Bishop Jeffery D. Thomas, Sr., Servant Pastor
Mount Rose Church
An Anointed Atmosphere
Dallas, TX 75249
www.mtrose.org

# Part One

## *Defilement to Deliverance*

Photo: Linda D. Lee

# 1

# My Soul Cried

Initially, I didn't call myself a whore…I'm sorry, I mean harlot. However, others could have, because over the years I slept with men I wasn't married to. That fact alone didn't keep me from attending church or working in ministries. I just added more ministries to my repertoire and hid behind my church persona.

It's funny how we perceive ourselves one way while others perceive us another way. If people really knew what was going on behind closed doors, they would be shocked. And I'm not just referring to *my* closed door. I'm also referring to the church, as you will see.

My former pastor, Roy Elton Brackins, Pastor/Founder of Grace Tabernacle Missionary Baptist Church, Forest Hill, Texas, said something so profound on October, 29, 2006. In his sermon, which he fed us every Wednesday and Sunday, he stated, "now it's time for some of us to learn how to cook for ourselves." At that time I didn't realize how much his comment affected me. But it was another sign received during those months that confirmed my assignment from the Lord. The Holy Spirit showed me…that *it was time* to share my testimony in order to help someone else heal and be delivered from their sexual demons, generational curses or strongholds tied to sexual sin.

I remember, on multiple occasions, Pastor Brackins delivering messages from Acts Chapter 1 and Acts 2:1-6. Verses 4-6 say, *"And they were all filled with the Holy Spirit and began to speak with other tongues, as the Spirit gave them utterance. And there were dwelling in Jerusalem Jews, devout men, from every nation under heaven. And when this sound occurred, the multitude came together, and were confused, because **everyone heard them speak in his own language.**"*

In a moment, I'm going to take his advice and share my predestined testimony. But most importantly, I have to speak, or deliver, the spiritual food in my own way in order to reach other people that may interpret the message their own way.

People receive messages in many different ways. So, some of this food may be broken down so much that a baby can understand it. If your spiritual understanding is on a higher level, then you will understand what I'm stating without my extra emphasis. Please bear with me if my elaboration gets too elementary for you. But, it would be ignorant and immature of me to try and impress you with large biblical or vocabulary words when I normally speak with simplicity.

Before you begin reading, let me warn you first- hand. If you are so sanctified, holy and spiritual that you are out of touch with what's really going on in some churches today, this book *may not* be for you. Some statements may be too graphic for your reading. However, in order for the Lord to effectively use me as a vessel to help someone through their deliverance, I need to call the sin by its name. Unfortunately, some of these names aren't mentioned in most churches. So, let me apologize in advance if the names of these demons or spirits offend you.

This book isn't meant to openly offend or condemn anyone. It is only one small tool that will open the door for seasoned saints, not babes in Christ, to have honest confession of their sins. It's time out for playing church! In the end, God will get all the glory from your deliverance.

Some people will read the title and assume *Snake* refers to men. Come on ladies, if you've ever been hurt by a man you automatically thought the same thing. Part of that thought is true and part of that thought isn't. I have to come to the defense of men, however, because women can also be *Snakes* and we can also share some of the same sexual demons as men. As women, we have the cleverness to be as mischievous as men. Let me repeat that: **As women, we have the cleverness to be as mischievous as men.**

*Random House Webster's Dictionary* also defines "snake" as a treacherous person…and treacherous means, "likely to betray trust, deceptive, untrustworthy or dangerous." I didn't read in either definition a reference to gender, did you? Of course you didn't.

I know snakes and serpents are represented as demonic beings in the Bible. But as you will discover, my *Snake* was everything I allowed to enter my spirit that wasn't of God. My S*nake* started with viewing pornography and progressed over the years to areas of fornication, premarital sex, lust, and masturbation with and without sex toys.

My freaky nature was hidden behind my church persona. My unclean spirit may not have been a "Legion" as in Mark 5: 8-9 (KJV), but there was more than one demon or spirit causing havoc in my life.

Over the years, these spirits entertained moods of anger, closet freakiness, depression, low self-esteem and debilitating self worth. I allowed negative forces to take over my thoughts and shackle my mind. To sum it up, I was weak. I took all those spirits and thoughts to bed with me, literally every night.

I want you to think about something. Take 10 minutes and read Mark 5. Put yourself in the place of the man from the tombs who was possessed with the "Legion" of spirits. Now, take out a piece of paper and write down your unclean spirits or demons. Before you start, let me give you some definitions: 1. Demon: an evil spirit; a wicked or cruel person. Random House Webster's Dictionary. *Richards Bible Dictionary* states a demon is an evil spiritual being, hostile to God and to humanity. 2. Spirit: a supernatural being. Webster. 2a. The part of the person's being thought of as the center of life, the will, thinking, feeling; that part of the man that survives death. New King James Concordance. Now, write down what has a stronghold on YOU?

What issue(s) did you THINK you had dealt with but, in reality, the issue(s) is still dealing with you? It is something you can't seem to shake off? If your issue isn't of the sexual nature, is it a paternal curse? Ok, your time is up. Now review what YOU wrote on your paper. Look at it real close because that's your "Legion". And, in case you couldn't think of anything, I don't know anyone that doesn't have one issue they're still trying to completely get over.

My legion was fornication, masturbation, pornography, childhood fondling, rape, sex-toys, erotic behavior and moods of freakiness.

As a young child, my curiosity about intimacy led to some compromising situations that I kept suppressed in my mind for years. I felt I was learning something that would make me "special" or "mature" when it came to relationships with men. But as the ole folks would say, I became an educated fool!

I was too young to understand the severity that this exposure would have in my life later on. Also, I was too young to understand that once those demon seeds had been planted in my spirit, they would later progress into other areas of my life. Meaning, one thing lead to another from a young age and continued into my adulthood. All because I was curious, needed more paternal attention and guidance, didn't understand intimacy and craved commitment. That was a bad combination of issues!

I had allowed my demon filled flesh to be infatuated

...................

*When the unclean spirit goes out of a man, he goes through dry places, seeking rest, and finds none. Then he says, I will return to my house from which I came. And when he comes, he finds it empty, swept, and put in order. Then he goes and takes with him seven other spirits more wicked than himself, and they enter and dwell there; and the last state of that man is worse than the first.*

Matthew 12:43-45 (NKJV)

with satisfying fleshly men instead of developing an intimate relationship with my Heavenly Father. From this point on, when I state, "I had an intimate relationship with the wrong man," understand that I am referring to the fleshly man vs. our Heavenly Father, which equals being in love with the wrong man. This concept can also be applied if you're a man and have an intimate relationship with a woman not sanctioned by God.

People with similar issues are too often scared to seek the church body's help because church folks have forgotten that we *all* have sinned. We tend to be judgmental of other people's sin, but not our own. There's no big sin or little sin. No sin is greater than the other. **Sin is sin!**

A lot of times we keep things in the closet and choose not to share them. We don't want anyone to know what had to be expunged from our slate. We don't want people to lose respect for us. I was one of those people. I was ashamed and embarrassed by some of my past. For many years, I allowed other people's opinions of my relationships to paralyze my future…until now.

The Lord placed it in my spirit to write this book from a realistic approach. It was time to reach seasoned saints that resembled me after being in church for many years, saved,

......................

*So set yourselves apart to be holy, for I, the Lord, am your God.*

Leviticus 20:7 (NLT)

served in ministry, not converted and a Christian "freak" after the benediction. Or, as 1 Corinthians 6 lists: *fornicator,* idolater, adulterer, homosexual, sodomite, thief, covetous, drunkard, reviler and extortioner. I was included in this list.

If you didn't know how wide spread sexual immorality is in our churches today, you do now. There are many newspaper articles that back up how wide spread sexual immorality is today. It is running rampant in all areas of our churches, behind closed doors, of course. Some churches are past the point of being called a "hot mess." They are starting to resemble a new generation Sodom and Gomorrah. **Enough is enough!**

The Holy Spirit didn't lead me to write this book because he wanted me to bash men or pastors or to embarrass my family or expose anyone. He wanted me to write this book as verifiable proof of his continued deliverance from *our* sins. If he delivered me, just imagine what he can do for you or someone you may know.

Later, I will elaborate on how the Lord used my procrastination against me in 2006. He'd already sent me signs that I needed to be delivered from these demons, especially fornication. But I moved tooooooooo slowwwwww. We all know what happens to you when you move too slow at heeding a message from God…he whips you real good.

..................

*For he chose us in him before the creation of the world to be holy and blameless in his sight.*

Ephesians 1:4 (NIV)

7

Do you remember the worse whipping you received from your mother or father? Well, if it was anything like the whipping I received from my mother…it left a lasting impression across my rear end. Just imagine receiving a whipping three or ten times worse than that one. This is what the Lord had in store for me when I moved too slow into my deliverance.

He perfectly positioned my fornicating partner, *Secret Fire*, to slowly unlock some of my suppressed issues linked through sexual seeds, passed on by a generational curse. I am sure you know what happens when Pandora's Box is opened.

The Lord used that opportunity to shake up my relationship with my son, family and Secret Fire, in order to unleash revelations the Holy Spirit had for me. You will soon understand how the Lord used that same stronghold tied to those demons that kept me hostage, to eventually set me free.

This plan first included removing some people from my life and surrendering to his will, and then everything else fell into place. If you had or are having any type of battle with a sexual demon, this book is for you. Even if you aren't wrestling with any of the issues I will discuss, he can still deliver you from whatever situation is currently plaguing you.

If I can assist *one* person through their healing deliverance process, then I have completed the assignment my Heavenly Father has given me.

. . . . . . . . . . . . . . . . . . .

*For God did not call us to be impure, but to live a holy life.*

1 Thessalonians 4:7 (NIV)

Follow me while I deliver the chapters of my predestined testimony as subjects the Lord placed in my spirit. Let me elaborate more extensively on how I let a small windstorm escalate into a hurricane over a matter of time. How many of you can say you survived a hurricane with only a few cuts and bruises? Well, I can!

Do you remember in John 4 when Jesus told the Samaritan woman at Jacob's well all about herself, her five husbands and informed her that the one she had now wasn't her own? If you continue reading in (v.28 NKJV), *"The woman then left her water pot, went her way into the city, and said to the men,* (v.29) *come, see a man who told me all things that I ever did. Could this be the Christ?"* Well, I know it was Christ. And, He is still alive and well today. Consider me a New Breed Samaritan woman with a purpose to glorify the name of Jesus through my testimony.

Hold on…it's going to be a bumpy ride!

………………..

*The Lord hears the prayer of the righteous.*

Proverbs 15:29 (NIV)

# 2

# You Can Run
# But You Can't Hide

When the Lord placed this title in my spirit, I had mixed emotions. A part of me was excited that He wanted to use me to help someone through my testimony. Another part of me wanted to run and hide like Jonah. I wanted to share the news about writing this book with my younger sister, JoAnn. The part of me that wanted to take off running like Jonah wanted my sister to say… girl you're crazy…the Lord isn't going to use you to help someone else…you're not a writer.

But what she said brought tears to my eyes. Continuous words of encouragement flowed from her mouth like water. My teary-eyes were a reflection of the growth our relationship had taken over the years. We always had a good relationship growing up, but I always felt inferior to my sisters. I never felt I had anything valuable to offer them because our interests were so different, until now. JoAnn told me she was happy for me. "You do what the Lord is leading you to do." Her words encouraged me to birth bits and pieces of this journey that night. I told her I didn't know where to start. She told me not to worry about the beginning or ending of the book, just to start writing. And I did what she said. I saw the Lord start constructing my spiritual womb to give birth to his Godly purpose.

Once I surrendered to his will, He began working in the secret cavities of my body. So, let me be a witness to you. If the Lord is leading you to do something, just do it. If you don't, he will keep that issue in front of you until you follow the vision, mission, assignment, instruction, direction or purpose he has for your life. It is a sign of obedience. Or, He may keep the issue in front of you because you *haven't* passed the test to move on. He already knew I was good at starting some assignments and not finishing them.

One afternoon, He sent me manna from heaven that fell on my job ... I usually didn't get too many unannounced visitors to my office. But that day was different. Out of nowhere, Mr. Ford stopped by my office because he had a gift for me. Even though I was happy to see him, I was surprised that he brought me a gift and a beautiful card.

. . . . . . . . . . . . . . . . . .

*Now the word of the Lord came to Jonah the son of Amittai, saying, "Arise, go to Nineveh, that great city, and cry out against it; for their wickedness has come up before Me." But Jonah arose to flee to Tarshish from the presence of the Lord.*

Jonah 1:1-3 (NKJV)

We had a cordial relationship, but there was something different about this visit. It seemed to be more serious than any other visit in the past. There was calmness in the air. For some reason I felt totally relaxed and at ease. It almost appeared dreamlike, as if we were in the middle of nowhere and there was a light hazed silhouette around the upper part of his body. I felt like time had stopped. Usually, when time appears to have stopped, we need to stop and listen for Gods voice in the atmosphere, which I did.

Our voices seemed to echo off my office walls. I could feel something indescribable in the air. Let me paint a picture so you will understand...

From the first day I met Mr. Ford he seemed special to me. He was quiet, anointed, soft spoken and always humble. Every time I was around him I treated him like E.F. Hutton. I leaned on his every word. Well, on this day I believe the spirit of the Lord made it crystal clear in written revelation. He used Mr. Ford as a messenger to deliver his word to me in the form of a card.

I'm a person that loves surprises, so the anticipation was building inside me to uncover the mystery behind the spontaneous visit and gift. I believe he knew the card would impact me emotionally. So he asked me to read it after he left my office, and I did. There was a blessing in my obedience

..................

*A friend loveth at all times, and a brother is born for adversity.*

Proverbs 17:17 (KJV)

13

*Covered*

to Mr. Ford. He didn't know the card would confirm God's purpose for my life.

You never know when the Lord is going to use someone or something to deliver a message from Him. Let me share how God manifested his revelation. Keep in mind, Mr. Ford and I saw each other every once in a while because we worked in separate buildings.

I hadn't shared with him much about my life other than that I wrote poetry from time to time. Let me paint a visual picture of the card.

Front of card:

*What lies behind us*

*and what lies before us*

*are tiny matters*

*compared to what lies within us.*

— Ralph Waldo Emerson

.....................

*I wait for you, O Lord; you will answer, O Lord my God.*

Psalm 38:15 (NIV)

Right inside cover of the card:

*I believe you have*

*Everything you need inside*

*To make it through.*

Now, here is the eloquently handwritten message Mr. Ford blessed me with on the left side of the card:

*Linda,*

*May God's favor be with you*

*and your family through your own*

*journey in this valley we call "life".*

*Do your part and allow God to*

*do the rest. I'll continue to*

*be one of your biggest fans.*

*God Bless and take care.*

*Mr. Ford   10-9-06*

I shared this personal message with you because I had been in prayer prior to Mr. Ford's visit for the Lord to reveal my purpose with clarity. You never know who, what or when the Lord will use to assist you in your spiritual growth. So be careful when entertaining strangers.

They could be an angel or messenger sent by God! I thank my Lord and Saviour Jesus Christ for using Mr. Ford, my guardian angel, as a vessel to manifest his word on that day. I truly believe that was one of a few life-altering moments for me.

My soul was happy and I was finally feeling some real joy. My mind was on over load from trying to receive all the messages the Holy Spirit was sending my way … I had to scream the name of Jesus when he sent me further confirmation of my purpose with two messages that following week. Both messages focused on listening to the Holy Spirit's direction for your purpose or assignment.

*My Purpose:*
*Use my testimony*
*to assist others through their season of healing*
*using my gift of compassion and encouragement.*
*My assignment:*
*Use my written testimony*
*globally to reach souls that desire*
*deliverance from sexual demons.*

. . . . . . . . . . . . . . . . . . . . . . .

If a person can be excited and scared at the same time, I was. I had more questions than answers. I asked Lady Brackins a question at Women's Ministry that week. I wanted to know how much of your testimony do you reveal if the Holy Spirit is leading you to put it in writing? In her calm eloquent voice she explained to me, "You will know how much … the Lord will lead you." When I returned home that night the spirit of the Lord reminded me of two scriptures:

> *Oh, taste and see that the Lord is good;*
> *Blessed is the man who trusts in Him!*
> *Oh, fear the Lord, you His saints!*
> *There is no want to those who fear Him.*
> *The young lions lack and suffer hunger;*
> *But those who seek the Lord*
> *Shall not lack any good thing.*

Psalm 34:8-10 (NKJV)

…………

> *For we walk by faith, not by sight.*

2 Corinthians 5:7 (NKJV)

People that really know me will tell you how emotional, sensitive and sentimental I can be at times. It doesn't take much for tears to fall from my eyes. So, you will understand when I say I started crying after reading Mr. Ford's card. I could finally stop running from my past to help someone in the future. They were tears of joy because I knew God sent Mr. Ford to hand deliver those words. Herein is what the Lord birthed in me.

17     *Covered*

# 3

## *From Devastation...*

As a youth, it wasn't easy being the middle child. I always felt I didn't receive the attention I thought I deserved. I felt something was missing, but I couldn't put my finger on it. I believe my late grandmother could read the lost look on my face. But no one ever talked to me about what I was feeling. Society calls this "Middle Child Syndrome." Even though my parents loved us, I felt they were too career oriented to give equal effective parental nurturing to all four children. Like most children, we all wanted equal quality time.

The military had my father's undivided attention and the ladder of success had my mom's attention. Don't misunderstand what I am saying. My parents always provided the things we needed, but I needed more personal attention. I craved attention! My heart felt something was always missing.

I wanted a modern day *Little House on the Prairie* home. I wanted my mother to come home from work, kiss all the kids and inquire into our school day. I anticipated my father's arrival from the flight line while the food was being placed on the table. In my dream, he would enter the kitchen and embrace my mother from behind with a peck on her cheek. With compassion in his heart, he would inquire whether she needed any help. For whatever reason, she'd always say no, and then turn to us for help. My father would return to the front door and remove his steel-toe boots. Of course, the couch always seemed to call his name shortly after his arrival. In between the time, he sat down on the couch till the setting of the dinner table and, of course ... he fell asleep.

It wouldn't take much for mom to wake him up. All she had to do was run her fingers through his hair. He knew instantly that it was dinner time. I know all of this sounds real good, but as I stated, it was a dream. Most of the time, our dinner time consisted of saying hello and good bye as we *passed* by the dinner table.

As far as my siblings, I felt lost in the shuffle while playing mediator between them. Many days and nights I felt mentally separated from my siblings; I was unheard and emotionally detached from everyone else. My mind drifted into early depression before I knew what the word meant. I battled with thoughts of my father favoring my older sister, Darlene. However, I couldn't figure out if this was because she was a Tom-Boy or because she resembled him more. Just when I thought things couldn't be worse, I began to feel in constant competition with my younger sister JoAnn. She

....................

*A wise child brings joy to a father; a foolish child brings grief to a mother.*

Proverbs 10:1 (NIV)

was the prettiest, smartest and most gifted of all the children. There weren't enough pedestals in the world for my mother to place her on.

Unfortunately, my brother, James, and I were the black sheep in the family. James got our parents' attention by trying to grow up too fast in the streets of Lake Como, Texas. I, on the other hand, received my black sheep title by becoming a bully so the boys from The Projects would stop picking on me.

My parents never knew I was scared to attend Elementary and Middle school some days. I believe they thought nothing was wrong because I was a popular child on the Air Force Base. But, I was being harassed because I was overweight at school and I took it out on kids from the base when I got home. I was under constant humiliation in school. If I wasn't being called "fat", "big butt" or "hippo", the kids would just laugh at me. No one had a clue that becoming a bully allowed me to release the anger that festered within. I also saw the power behind being a bully and used it to my advantage.

However, those teary nights didn't begin to scratch the surface of my real pain. I just wanted to FEEL loved. I heard some lovely words from my family, but I never felt completely connected to the love. You would think those feelings would fade as I got a little older. But they didn't.

...................

*A wise child accepts a parent's discipline; a young mocker refuses to listen.*

Proverbs 13:1 (NIV)

I still felt somewhat disconnected in middle school. Until one day my bus driver saw the hurt in my eyes and tried to comfort me with words. Little did I know, his concern wasn't as genuine as he pretended. What I had mistaken for genuine concern was his clever scheme to gain my confidence. He slowly elevated his compliments from, "You look nice today" to "You just let me know where you want to get dropped off today".

Of course I thought I was pretty special after receiving all that attention. I never put two and two together until it was too late. I remember one day he stopped at my bus stop and I got up from my seat. He looked in the driver's mirror as I approached the front door. Just as I reached his seat, he held out his hand as if he wanted me to slap his hand. Almost like giving him an ole-school "five," which I did. However, he didn't let my hand go quickly. I jerked away and ran off the bus. A couple of days later he did the same thing. But, this time he let my hand go and he put his around my waist as he chatted with me.

Not long after that incident, he asked if I wanted to make some money. After running off the bus I went home and thought about his statement. I was no different from most kids; I had already spent his money in my head. The only problem was I didn't know what I had to do to get the money. I remember finally asking him how much money he was talking

………………..

*Fools mock at sin, but among the upright there is favor.*

Proverbs 14:9 (NKJV)

about and what I had to do. I'm sure by now you have put two and two together ... he wanted to touch my chest for *one dollar*. Of course, being a child, I didn't think anything was wrong with it. So, I agreed to let him do it after the last child exited the bus. I remember that he drove slow as I kneeled beside his seat. As I reach into my suppressed memory bank, I specifically remember that he slid his right hand down the front of my shirt as he drove with his left hand. To my surprise, it was over as quick as it began. I really thought I was rich with that dollar.

Little did I know, that dollar was the beginning of my horror story. The bus driver enjoyed fondling me so much that he made the same offer again. And of course, being a naïve child, I accepted his offer. Unfortunately, in the middle of fondling me the second time, his offer changed. He offered me more money to touch my private area. I remember yelling "No!," quickly moving away from him and insisting he let me off the bus. He tried to get me to change my mind. I just kept saying, "Let me off the bus, let me off the bus!" He finally stopped, opened the door, and I ran past him. There was a brush of trees and bushes lining the road. I was too scared to go straight home, so I hid there for a few minutes.

. . . . . . . . . . . . . . . . . . . .

*I will refresh the weary and satisfy the faint.*

Jeremiah 31:25 (NIV)

By no means did I want my family to know what had happened, especially my father! See, my father is a quiet man and keeps to himself. But, he will hurt you for messing with his family. I can only imagine what he would have done if he knew a grown man had touched his daughter...I'm glad he didn't find out about that situation and me sneaking on other buses to go to school. However, the situation worked itself out when that driver was replaced. Like clockwork, a big sigh of relief came from me each day the school bus arrived. My heart stopped racing when I noticed HE wasn't in the driver seat.

Over time, my brother James and I wandered about, as if in a far country like the prodigal son in Luke 15: 11-32. Our far country was a little different than that of the prodigal son. We wandered into dark areas of life, not necessarily experienced by military brats. James was anxious to grow-up fast by experiencing life and I wanted to experience life fast in order to grow up. The ole folks would say I was "fass".

There was something about military life that felt restraining to me. I felt I was missing out on the outside world. It appeared the more we went to church on the south-side, the less I knew about real life. I wouldn't say we were sheltered. But, I believed there was a lot more to experience on the roads that led out the front gate and off the base.

...................

*You children must always obey your parents,*
*for this is what pleases the Lord.*

Colossians 3:20 (NLT)

Undoubtedly, I had reached my curious stage. I was curious about some things children my age shouldn't be concerned with. At the top of my curious list was: relationships, intimacy and in plain English…sex. So, I did what other curious young ladies my age did, I turned to young men for attention.

My parents' constantly saying, "keep your dress down and your legs closed", wasn't enough information for me anymore. Especially since the birds and the bees talk never came.

I knew in order to please young men I had to be more knowledgeable about life experiences. I didn't want to be like the other young ladies and be a *people pleaser*; I wanted to become an educated *man pleaser.* Here is an example…you know the cliché: "What it took to get him, it will take to keep him?" Well, that was constantly on my mind. My mind was wrapped up in the pleasure of pleasing men. Let's just say, I wanted to get them and keep them without a problem.

I will never forget the first time I was introduced to pornography. It was one summer afternoon and my parents were at work. The bathroom window was cracked. The birds were chirping in the tree outside the window. I had to use the restroom and there were only a few pieces of toilet paper left on the roll. So, I searched the shelves in the bathroom for another roll. I knew we stored extra rolls and other items on the shelf. Much to my surprise, the rolls weren't the only thing hidden way back on the shelf.

Being in middle school, my first thought was, "what are these?" They were adult magazines. My second thought was, "hmmm … let me check this out." I flipped through those pages and saw the advertisement for adult toys and clothes. I was instantly hooked on the whips, chains, edible lotions and fancy clothes!

The magazines captured my curiosity while answering some of the birds and the bees' questions at the same time. I felt like I had found a gold mine. And yes, I had had Health Education in school, but it didn't compare to the magazines I had just found. Those magazines came with enough pictures, articles and advertisement to secretly answer questions I couldn't ask my parents.

I have to admit, I enjoyed sneaking into the bathroom, locking the door and picking up where I left off last. I was very careful to hide the magazines in the exact spot, so I wouldn't get caught. Someone must have discovered my private viewing party, because one day the magazines disappeared from the shelf. Without a whisper or sound…they were gone.

Little did I know, as an intriguing youth, that viewing those magazines would introduce sexual demons (pornography, sex, intimacy, masturbation and sex toys) into my spirit, and I didn't know what most of those words meant. But, believe you me, I found out in high school what those words meant.

I will never forget dating my boyfriend Kel. One particular night, after his graduation, we wanted something else to do. We were trying to decide how to celebrate his special day. All his friends were making normal graduation plans. You

....................

*I sought the Lord, and he answered me; He delivered me from all my fears.*

Psalm 34:4 (NIV)

can read in between the lines and tell that Kel and I weren't normal. We jumped in the car and rode around Fort Worth trying to find something fun to do. It didn't take long before all of our fun ideas had run out ... then we saw some flickering lights in the distance.

We were approaching a XXX novelty store. There was something about those flickering lights that caught our attention. It didn't take much convincing from Kel for me to want to see what was inside. At the same time, we decided, "lets' do it".

We tried not to be conspicuous by quickly parking and entering the establishment. We maturely walked in and presented the clerk with our identification. Kel didn't seem nervous; however, I felt the need to escape to the restroom. I was really hoping he would change his mind about being there when I came out. Unfortunately, the gaze in his eyes made my wish impossible.

I could instantly tell he had visited that store before because he knew where everything was located. For some strange reason I was still jumpy and uneasy. I knew at any moment someone I knew would come through the door. He tried to ease my mind by saying, "Everybody's here for the same reason and it's going to be alright."

As my anxiety subsided, my senses heightened at all the toys in front of me. I now possessed the same gaze that he had in his eyes. At that moment, I wanted to see everything in the store and learn how to use the toys. Kel had something else in mind. He wanted to go upstairs to the theatre and play. Of course I thought he was just joking.

I quickly found out he wasn't. He was dead serious. Our synchronized steps toward the theater proved it. My surprise awaited me at the top of the stairs, behind two double doors.

It was a smoky, pitch black theatre that had a few sparse movie goers in attendance. As Kel and I located a seat, I could see couples performing sexual acts as if they were at home. I was shocked, embarrassed and vowed the make that my last visit to the theater…only, after Kel and I participated in some playing ourselves.

If you are keeping a time line you can see how fast my sexual seed grew. I went from adult magazines to adult stores, adult theater, XXX movies and sex toys linked to masturbation. The visit to the theatre backfired and didn't scare me away from learning more. It propelled me *into* learning different sex acts. After that, I started checking out books from the library on certain adult subjects and men's fantasies. Remember, I was trying to become an educated man pleaser.

What I learned excited me in many ways. And my well endowed bust-line excited young men in other ways. There were days when I felt a sense of relief because I learned something new that day. However, there was still a void within me that I couldn't explain.

Unfortunately, I didn't know my desire to be loved by a man would later develop into such a stronghold on my life. I learned this lesson the hard way when I met and dated another

………………..

*The Lord upholds all those who fall and lifts up all who are bowed down.*

Psalms 145:14 (NIV)

young man during my high school years—Tee. Nothing made me happier at that time than pleasing Tee. He was the only one that understood how on fire my body felt.

I remember bagging groceries at the base commissary one Saturday afternoon. A hot feeling came over me while I was working. I immediately started looking for Tee to provide some relief to my heated situation. He lived off base and no one had seen him get dropped off for work. I knew Tee was wrapped tightly around my finger and it wouldn't take much to push him over my way ... so I kept searching the commissary for him. And, out of nowhere, he appeared.

We took turns playing mental foreplay that day. I passed him in the commissary and brushed his leg on purpose. Later, he passed by me and accidentally touched me. I would then sneak up to him and whisper tender thoughts in his ear. His body movement was a perfect indication that I was messing with his mind. The same feeling that came over my body would illuminate over his face.

Shortly after, we would rendezvous out back and engage in a kissing and fondling session. Neither of us cared if we were caught or got our clothes dirty. We only cared about sharing an affectionate kiss or a simple embrace. We loved going to work because we knew our worlds would meet there.

..................

*For I, the Lord your God, am a jealous God, visiting the iniquity of the fathers upon the children to the third and fourth generations of those who hate Me, but showing mercy to thousands, to those who love Me and keep my commandments.*

Exodus 20:5b-6 (NKJV)

Our work atmosphere became our playground for quality time, since we attended different high schools.

You would have to know Tee to truly understand that statement. Tee was 5'6, 110 lbs, coco skin complexion, quiet and soft spoken. My body spoke the words he wanted to say. My heart not only fluttered at each touch, it stopped. Time seemed to stand still when he stepped into the commissary... and it would only start again when he left my side.

There was always tension in Tee's home. I believe I understood him better than his family. My parents didn't know it, but I thought I was in love with him. It could be because he showed me the attention I desired or filled the void my heart craved.

On more than one occasion, my eyes were focused on the wrong thing. This usually landed me in some compromising situations. One of which I never shared with Tee or my parents during our dating season. I can't recall the exact date of the incident, but I can recall the other information around that date.

After dating for some time, Tee began using drugs heavily, which put a strain on our relationship. Once I saw he wasn't going to change I decided to break up with him and go my separate way. I made sure other things occupied my time on the weekends to get Tee off my mind. One day our co-worker invited some of the baggers to his house party. Since I was still friends with Tee's sister, Mary, I asked if either of them were going to attend. I knew Mary would attend because she had a real reputation around town for being a party animal. My main reason for wanting to go was to see Tee and talk to him. I just wanted to touch him again.

A couple of days passed and Friday finally arrived. I knew Mary would be at work because Friday and Saturday were big money tip days at the commissary. Mary arrived and confirmed that she and Tee were going to the party. She offered me a ride; I accepted it thinking Tee would be riding with us. Later, she informed me that he would be arriving separately with his friend Darryl.

Mary and I coordinated our Saturday arrangements and her mother dropped us off at the party.

When we arrived, the party was jumping strong. The music was blasting and almost everybody was dancing. Mary and I split-up so she could work the room and I went looking for Tee. I found him, but he was preoccupied with his drugs, so I joined the party scene.

The party was still going strong into the wee hours of Sunday morning. I knew my curfew was fast approaching. So, I started looking for Mary to see when our ride was picking us up. She was nowhere to be found and the party was shutting down. Where do you think she was? You guessed it. Mary was gone, she had left the party with a man! The other guests were starting to leave too. I was standing around looking stupid and wondering how I was going to make curfew.

I had already missed curfew a few times being out with my softball team. I knew if I missed curfew this time my mother might unplug that extension cord and whip me good.

....................

*Hatred stirs up strife, but love covers all sins.*

Proverbs 10:12 (NKJV)

*Covered*

That's when reality hit me; I was stranded and too scared to call her.

I went outside to see if Mary had returned from her extracurricular activity. Outside, I ran into two of my classmates, Jimmy and Charles. Since Mary hadn't returned, they offered to take me home. However, they needed to make one stop first. I agreed because they assured my arrival home on time.

Jimmy drove and Charles was in the passenger seat. I rested my blurry eyes in the back seat and tried to figure out where we were going. The surroundings were not familiar to me. It appeared we were going in the opposite direction from my house. I asked them again, where are we going? They reminded me that they had to make a stop first, and then they would take me home.

After driving a while, Jimmy stopped at this house. He said he had to run in for a minute.

My mind was still trying to process who, what and where are we. So, Charles and I waited in the car. I looked at my watch; my curfew had passed. I started to panic and told Charles to go get Jimmy. He went in the house and he never came back.

Finally, I got out of the car and rang the door bell. Jimmy answered the door and explained that they had a problem. He

...................

*I will forgive their wickedness and will remember their sins no more,"*
*says the Lord.*

Hebrews 8:12 (NIV)

invited me in while trying to explain what was going on. I only heard half of his explanation because my mind was on getting home. I noticed Charles wasn't in the room, but it still didn't dawn on me what was going on.

I remember hearing the door lock and Charles finally emerged from another room. Jimmy decided to tell me the truth, "There is no real problem, but you have to have sex with us before we will take you home." Initially, I thought he was playing and I started laughing. But the look on their faces told a different story.

I told them I wasn't having sex with either of them and reached for the kitchen phone located on the wall. Jimmy jerked it out of my hand and unplugged it. I started for the front door and he blocked it. Charles was pacing behind me as if he was nervous. I told them to let me leave or let me call my parents for a ride. Jimmy said, "You don't even know where you are." And he was right. At that time, I didn't have a clue where I was.

I informed both of them what they were doing was wrong and "no" meant "no." I wasn't going to have intercourse with them or let them run a train on me. I started looking for another exit door. The only other door I saw led to a bedroom. Charles was blocking the opening to the hallway. I was cornered in

....................

*Let the wicked forsake his way and the evil man his thoughts. Let him turn to the Lord, and he will have mercy on him, and to our God, for he will freely pardon.*

Isaiah 55:7 (NIV)

the kitchen/ living room area. I started to double talk them as I slowly walked toward Charles and the hallway.

I approached Charles and tried to push my way past him. That didn't work. Charles was a strong football player. Jimmy figured out what I was doing, so he tackled me from behind as I wrestled with Charles. That tackle landed all of us in the bedroom. I yelled for help as they wrestled me onto the bed.

I kept yelling and kicking for them to stop as tears rolled down my face. Charles held my hands over my head and Jimmy proceeded to take my pants off. As Jimmy entered me first, Charles watched with anticipation. I don't remember at what point I gave up fighting and just laid there limp.

Not in a million years would I have thought two of my classmates would rape me. I fell into that same mental trap as other rape victims, I blamed myself for years. I couldn't bring myself to tell my parents. So, I just took my punishment when I finally returned home.

It didn't take much to suppress what happened while continuing my school functions. However, I had to develop a clever way of avoiding Jimmy and Charles for the rest of the year. Some classmates wondered why I started being rude to them. If they only knew...the secret was on the tip of my tongue many times.

Again you see, a different type of sexual seed was planted in my spirit. Later, you will meet Secret Fire who unlocked these suppressed memories and some other unresolved hurt.

Years later, when I heard Kirk Franklin confess on national TV that he was addicted to porn for many years, I felt his pain. I saw similarities in his confession and what I experienced as a youth. I didn't believe I was an addict nor did I consider calling myself an addict. Mainly because I felt there was something ugly tied to that word. It sounded dirty and filthy. And, once again, I didn't see myself in either of those words.I remember one night my spiritual sister, Sis. Mary Rhodes, was ministering to me after reading an excerpt from this book. She asked me an important question, "If you didn't consider yourself an addict, what do you think an addict is?" She proceeded to state, "An addict does some of the same things you were doing by sneaking around to get your high or fix at the adult store." Then, a light went off in my head. I was drawn to some of those demons linked to porn for a different reason. I believe some men are drawn to the visual aspect of porn.

They're captivated by a simple visual desire of seeing their fantasy played out on film. Some women are drawn to it to learn how to pleasure their mate, how to fulfill a fantasy while retaining his attention. I'm sorry to say, during this learning period I wasn't thinking about the scriptures. That's why it was so easy for me to do the complete opposite of what the word said.

Shamefully, I had defiled my body and the name of God with my actions. My curiosity of those demons was the beginning of my storm. However, one relationship in particular set more wheels in motion.

I tried really hard not to add this to the book. I knew it related, but I still didn't want to face the truth of the matter, I really wanted to forget what happened. I guess you're wondering, "What is she talking about?" Let me elaborate.

I got a call in July 2009 from one of my spiritual sisters. She explained how rough her day had been, until she accepted an invitation to a birthday celebration. Not long after she arrived at the event, the guest of honor shared her disappointment from being in a relationship with a brother on the *DL.

Everyone noticed a countenance of hurt lingering on her face. Sister gleaned with great anticipation because she heard many similarities to my testimony. At that moment my name dropped in her spirit. She knew I could minister to the honoree.

It was time to let my taboo secret out of the bag and minister to somebody.

Only a hand full of people knew of my marriage to a DL brother over 20 years ago. And Sister was one of them.

. . . . . . . . . . . . . . . . .

*Bear with each other and forgive whatever grievances you may have against one another. Forgive as the Lord forgave you.*

Colossians 3:13 (NIV)

---

***Down-Low (DL) brother:*** *Undercover male in a relationship with people of both genders. Sometimes he's married and confused about his sexual preference. Usually he claims to be heterosexual, but straddles the fence as a closet bi-sexual or has bi-curious tendencies. In the end, he is fully transformed into a homosexual. However, in some cases, he is homosexual from the start and still in the closet. Due to society's lifestyle opinions, he is scared to come out of the closet until the pressure becomes unbearable.* ***(Self-defined)***

Somehow she felt sharing my DL experience would begin a healing process for the honoree if she received what I had to say.

When I spoke with the honoree I instantly discerned that she wasn't completely ready to receive what I had to say. She lingered in her healing process between guilt and forgiveness. Her feelings of guilt were tied to other physical abuses from her childhood. Coincidently, she was more inclined to forgive her recent partner of his deceit. So, I shared my DL experience.

I met Mitch while attending trade school. He was different compared to most of the other men I met at school. He was a few years older than me. He was slender, soft spoken with a quiet spirit. I could tell he was a hard working country boy. After a few conversations with him I could also tell he was a high achiever. We grew closer as each day turned into weeks and weeks into months.

Then came a day when he had to tell me that he would be graduating soon. I, of course, had many semesters remaining in my trade. The reality of his comment hurt and I immediately felt abandoned. I started wondering if I would ever see him again.

It wasn't hard for him to read my facial expression either. In a calm voice he said, "I will send for you, we will still be together." So, I took him at his word. And he didn't lie.

We kept dating after he graduated and became great friends. One day there was a knock at my dorm room door. The voice said, "Linda you have a phone call." It was a call I will never forget. It was Mitch calling to check on me and see how my grades were coming along. Then he invited me to come visit and meet his family. Over the next few weeks, we made all the arrangements and I eventually arrived in his home town. Now let me fast forward.

Our relationship was wonderful; we dated another year or so, fell in love and later married after I graduated. We moved to his hometown and lived temporarily in his grandmother's old house. Little did I know, my own 'Little House on the Prairie' moment was getting ready to turn into a horror story.

After the birth of my son, Mitch informed me that he had previously experienced a *bi-curious* moment with two so-called friends that lived in town. I didn't believe him at first, but came to my senses quickly. He convinced me that it was a one-time thing and would never happen again. He also reiterated that he wasn't gay. Being a young wife and mother, what did I know? Military life never exposed me to any situation like that. So, the way I was raised, you took a person at their word. And that's what I did.

After I finished crying and trying to make sense of everything, I tried hard to forget his confession to me.

Unfortunately, he had another secret that he didn't disclose until after we divorced.

Sometime later, we moved from his hometown to Fort Worth, Texas and temporarily lived with my parents. It didn't take long for us to find our own place and start a new life. He found a great job working at night and I worked during the day. His co-workers always invited him out for a beer after work. He always declined. One night, however, he reconsidered their invitation. When he called during his break he sought my approval. I didn't have a problem with it because he deserved a night out with the fellas. He did exactly what he said he would do; he went and had a few beers and came home. He made this request a few more times, but the last time... he didn't come home.

I paged him a few times but received no response. Finally, I heard his keys in the door. I waited with anticipation to hear his explanation for not coming home. Sooooon as he walked in the door I could tell he had been with another woman. He looked guilty as charged. The more I questioned him, the more he acted as if he *didn't* owe me an explanation. At that point I knew I would have to snoop to get my answers. Warning: Don't snoop, unless you are ready for the truth!

I waited till he went to sleep and went through his wallet. I know, I know, that is a big "no no".

Anyway, I found what I was looking for. Folded in his wallet was a small piece of paper with a woman's name and number on it. And yes, I called her.

Back in the 80's I don't know a woman that wouldn't have done the same thing. Well anyway, I got her on the phone. Of course she said she didn't know Mitch and hung up in my face.

But a few minutes later, the phone rang. A male voice said, "You called my sister asking about Mitch?" I said, "Yes I did." He said, "Mitch isn't dating my sister...HE'S DATING ME!!!!!" The phone and room became silent. My mouth dropped and my heart sunk. I was in shock and felt comatose.

Not long after that disclosure, I came home to discover Mitch had left Martell and I for his lover. Martell had just begun walking. Now, I was faced with sharing my son with his bisexual father and his lover while trying to regain respect for myself as a woman. Could you have handled this situation as a young parent? What would've gone through your mind outside of physically hurting the person? Well, I can say my mind was *gone*. I didn't know what to think at that point. Everything I thought I knew was questionable and everything I believed to be true was unfolding as a lie.

The thought of getting an HIV/AIDS test hadn't entered my mind. My focus was on taking care of my son and gaining some dignity back in myself.

While dealing with his demons, I didn't know mine laid dormant ready to explode. Nor did I know I would later be dealing with my own tri-fold generational curse and stronghold linked to my father and son.

Prior to my next serious relationship, my self-esteem was non-existent. I struggled with existence and questioned my *worth as a woman*. I replayed our marriage in my head many days and nights, in an attempt to understand what I did wrong.

I cooked, cleaned, worked and satisfied all of his intimate needs. I was loving, compassionate, supportive and submissive. Yes, I nagged some and complained a little, but that couldn't be it.

What happened? I blamed myself. When no answer seemed to make sense, I decided to *prove* I was still desirable

....................

*Trouble chases sinners, while blessings chase righteous.*

Proverbs 13:21 (NLT)

to men. I journeyed into one relationship after another, trying to prove to myself that I could trust again.

It was scary to know that I really couldn't trust people. My mind started playing tricks on me while my heart was shattered into unrecognizable pieces.

Much later, there came a point when Mitch moved into his own place. During Martell's visits, I took the opportunity to flirt with him. I still wasn't convinced that he didn't desire me anymore, so I offered my body to him. He accepted my advances. Again, on the next visit, I offered my body to him. He accepted. It was during the following visit when he informed me that he was no longer bisexual, but fully homosexual. I left his apartment so shattered I didn't know what to do.

The thought of getting an HIV/AIDS test crossed my mind, but embarrassment prevented me from going.

To this day, I believe if the Lord didn't have his hand on me, I would've lost my mind. I was truly in the mental fight of my life. But thank God, He reached down and grabbed me before I went over the edge. First, He reminded me that my son needed me. Then, He reminded me that I didn't do anything wrong as a wife. I understood at that point that homosexuality was a *choice* Mitch made!

Here's another fast forward that shows God's awesome power. Mitch ran through men like water. However, during

.....................

*A gentle answer turns away wrath, but harsh words stir up anger.*

Proverbs 15:1 (NIV)

his so-called relationships, physical abuse seemed to occur. And who do you think they called for help? You guessed it, me. They would call me at 2 or 3 a.m. to defuse their argument or fight. I became their personal counselor and confidante.

Even though I felt awkward, being the ex-wife, I listened and explained that I didn't condone their relationship. Within seconds, I proceeded to minister and counsel them about getting back in church, etc. At that moment God used me as a vessel to speak to them.

Even though I had my own issues while straddling the fence, the Lord brought back to my remembrance enough word to speak on His behalf. But in my quiet time I started praying for their deliverance from homosexuality.

I tried constantly to abandon Mitch's world and focus on my own relationship. But my trust in men was gone. Either I helped sabotage the relationships or the men lacked the integrity to continue dating. That was my sign to pack quickly like the children of Israel and head toward the promise land. Once I crossed my Red Sea I would say, "Whewww! Thank God I'm not in that situation anymore."

My problem was that I didn't learn the lesson and instead, repeated a vicious cycle while dating. It wasn't enough to move into a relationship with a momma's boy; I had to graduate over the years into a relationship with a physical abuser, closet alcoholic and Pastor living a triple life (not double).

. . . . . . . . . . . . . . . . . . .

*You shall not lie with a male as with a woman. It is an abomination.*

Leviticus 18:22 (NKJV)

Even though I almost gave up dating after that relationship, I regained my senses enough to get my first HIV/AIDS test. It was negative, thank God. He spared me from all disease and STD's. That day I promised myself I would get tested every six months or so to keep my conscience clear.

I was constantly in and out of toxic relationships that were killing me slowly. The poison wasn't a chemical substance bought on the street. It was a fluid produced in the male reproductive organs, called semen.

Millions of spermatozoa (sperm) in the semen became a hallucinogenic narcotic to my soul. I didn't realize how powerful this drug was, until I uncovered that the common denominator in each relationship was fornication, premarital sex and soul ties. And semen was discovered at each crime scene.

Just like He delivered me from this cycle, He can deliver you. The question is: How bad do you want to be delivered? You have to be past the point of just talking about it and be proactive in doing something about it.

For many years I struggled to understand who I was and why I was the way I was. Why did I feel so needy? Why did I desire attention from men? What was it about *hearing* a man say "I love you" that seduced my mind? It wasn't until later in life that the light bulb finally went off, the Holy Spirit

...................

*Let there be no sexual immorality, impurity, Or greed among you.*

Ephesians 5:3 (NLT)

revealed that these actions were all linked to a generational curse and family secret.

In 2007, I decided that I needed to do a self evaluation to discover these answers. What I "uncovered" didn't surprise me; it only confirmed what I already felt. I wasn't the only family member living in secret sin! Each paternal connection exemplified traits and chromosomes of this same behavior at some point. Now, all the pieces to my life were starting to make more sense for my deliverance.

A key step in pursuing deliverance is bringing your problem to the Lord. Your healing won't be complete until you verbally bring it before the Lord. You can say all day that you have been healed from any incident or situation. In my opinion, if you can't verbally speak about the experience, you haven't been healed. That is like saying, "I forgive you but I won't forget." Then you haven't truly forgiven."

Please let your past scars heal so you can receive your blessing that's waiting on the other side. Sometimes your blessing is linked to your healing and forgiveness. Your blessing is waiting on you to do the same thing…heal and forgive.

It was plain and clear that the Lord had placed me in an observation mode as part of my journey. He wanted me to observe all the relationships around me to locate the answers

. . . . . . . . . . . . . . . . . . . .

*We can make our plans, but the Lord determines our steps.*

Proverbs 16:9 (NLT)

to my questions. Then, he provided divine intervention and quietly dissolved some of those relationships.

When I say the Holy Spirit came in my house like a tornado, please believe it. Every important relationship was shaken up. The communication with my son was disturbed, my relationship with my family was like walking on pens and needles, and my relationship with Secret Fire had rumbled to a boiling point. I thought my life was spinning out of control.

The Lord allowed me to experience those storms so that I can share them with you. I know you're wondering what all of this has to do with *In Bed with a Snake*. Well, remember when I told you to keep the definition of 'defiled' in your mind? Recall the definition while visualizing me taking those storms to bed with me every night.

Please allow the Holy Spirit to show you like He showed me that before you can truly be loved by anyone...you must first love Him, then yourself.

Remember these key points:

- **Delight yourself in him**
  Psalm 37:4
  Delight yourself also in the Lord, and He shall give you the desires of your heart.

- **Understand the definition of love**
  1 John 4:8
  God is love
  Real love does not hurt.

- **Understand the misuse of clichés**

  Proverbs 31: 10-31
  I want a virtuous woman

  Read Chapter: 9,
  Virtuous - defined

  Genesis 1-27
  I desire a Godly man

  Read Chapter: 10, Traits of a Godly man <u>before</u> he sinned

.....................

*If you search for good, you will find favor; but if you search for evil, it will find you.*

Proverbs 11:27 (NLT)

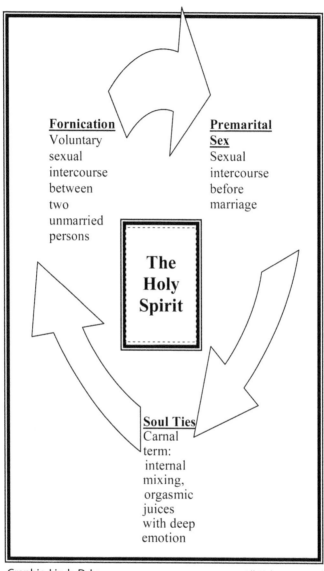

**Fornication**
Voluntary sexual intercourse between two unmarried persons

**Premarital Sex**
Sexual intercourse before marriage

**The Holy Spirit**

**Soul Ties**
Carnal term: internal mixing, orgasmic juices with deep emotion

Graphic: Linda D. Lee

. . . . . . . . . . . . . . . . . . . .

*You can't heal until you forgive your past.*

# 4

# ... To God's Revelation

I'm not a person that dreams a lot and recalls the details. However, I do remember three important dreams over the course of my life. Two of which are relevant now. In my teens, I had a dream about wrestling in bed with a snake. By no means did I understand the dream. Nor did I tie the dream with me being a "fass" young lady. I only took the dream to be what it was, a dream where a real snake was in bed with me. And for some strange reason, we started wrestling. However, as quick as the dream appeared…it disappeared.

Sweat beads were the only remnants of the dream that remained when I came to my senses. But due to the anxiety of that experience, I never told my parents or anyone about the dream. I have to admit; the dream scared me, but didn't have any meaning at that time. You better believe I looked over my shoulder and around corners for awhile though. Over the years, the dream slowly faded from the surface of my memory. It laid dormant in the crevice of my mind.

Now, let me fast forward and connect the initial dream to the rest of my life.

Back in July of 2004, I met a wonderful gentleman online. We were both members of a networking site that catered to minorities. I used my personal page to meet new people and post poetry. However, I knew there was a chance I would be contacted by men on a personal level. Or, even make some unusual contacts with my poetry, which I did.

I was fortunate to meet many people from different states and countries. Some wanted me to post my poems on their sites while others wanted to inquire into my dating status. I will never forget receiving a message on July 2, 2004 from one gentleman in particular; let's call him "Secret Fire". His message quickly caught my attention because it was short, to the point and left my mind wondering.

I finally stopped by his personal page to learn more about him. I remember he was playing the drums in the first picture. In other pictures he posed with Stellar Award-winning gospel artists and other acclaimed musicians. My mind was so suspicious that, I contacted him to see who he really was, or pretended to be. I'd gotten used to the façade people portrayed online. But my curiosity got the best of me.

I could tell there was something behind that light caramel complexion, six-four stature and thick physique. I didn't know what it was though. But even through the computer I could tell he had naturally wavy hair and impeccably white teeth. He had sex appeal that I couldn't explain. I was definitely open to exploring more of him.

Immediately, Fire and I started communicating on and off the personal site – before the ink was dry on his divorce papers, might I add. He quickly let me know he was a slow typist and wanted to communicate more by phone. That was fine with me because I enjoyed talking on the phone. We talked for hours at a time and often into the next morning. We were both curious about each other's lifestyle, among other things. He wanted to know more about my position with the government and I wanted to know more about his experience playing percussion in gospel plays and being an assistant record producer.

Even though I only told him basic information about myself, he openly shared his upcoming travel itinerary. He would be departing in a few months for Arkansas on family business and later return to the tour circuit.

Soon enough, the time came when I finally felt comfortable enough to meet him in person. It was purely coincidental that my 39th birthday had just passed. My mind was still riding high because I usually celebrate my birthday all month. But, I calmed down enough to accept his invitation to meet over the weekend in Fort Worth, Texas. I thought it would be nice to finally meet face to face. However, there was one problem. Not many eating establishments stayed open after his play rehearsal. So, our choices were limited to a local restaurant.

..................

*A person without self-control is as defenseless as a city with broken-down walls.*

Proverbs 25:28 (NLT)

I don't believe he could hear the nervousness in my voice as we finalized the date. But, I knew I needed to mentally prepare for our first meeting. Especially, since I wanted to appear confident, relaxed and attentive. Each day that passed brought more anxiety and increased deep breaths. Yes, I talked to him daily, but all of that was pushed aside for the physical meeting.

Saturday night finally arrived and it was time for our date. I anticipated that he would arrive late from Dallas and that I would become nervous waiting on him. Much to my surprise, he had arrived early and waited for me in the parking lot. I said, "hmmm…" as I pulled up next to his car. I really was surprised that he beat me there, since I lived in town. At that moment, I knew he was just as anxious to meet as I was. I tried not to show any excitement; it was too early for all that. As I exited my car he remained in his, finalizing some business arrangements. I waited patiently for him so I could put a face with his voice.

Little to my surprise, he quietly exited his car and immediately solved part of the mystery.

Do you remember the story of David and Goliath, how David was so little compared to Goliath?

Well, that is how I felt when Fire got out of his car and stood next to me. I stood at 5´6, shoulder length hair,

..................

*The Lord's searchlight penetrates the human spirit, exposing every hidden motive.*

Proverbs 20:27 (NLT)

voluptuous figure, adorned with French vanilla scents and toe rings that accented my outfit.

He, on the other hand, looked just like his picture online, youthful. But the picture didn't reveal his smooth skin, beautiful smile, pierced ear and extra-thick physique. All I could do is look up at him as he repeated his famous line, "What's up Cover?"

Even though he looked and smelled good, the other half of his personality was hidden behind his dark shades, overconfident attitude and almost cocky demeanor.

After we embraced with a hug, we quickly moved the introduction inside the restaurant. We were given the best seat in the house…which looked just like every other seat.

Almost every seat was available; after all, it was the wee hours of the morning. As I sat across the table from him, I still felt the need to get past his façade. Oh yes, there was still something mysterious about him and the shiny object in his mouth. I hate to admit, but my mind drifted in and out of the conversation, because the object in his mouth kept distracting me.

I waited patiently for Fire to tell me what it was. Unfortunately, he was taking too long. So, I popped what turned out to be the big question of the night, "What is that in your mouth…is it a tongue ring?" After he finished chuckling

………………..

*The wise are glad to be instructed, but babbling fools fall flat on their faces.*

Proverbs 10:8 (NLT)

in a sexy way he said, "wellllll, yes it is." Right then and there I knew I had met a big WIDE-OPEN freak and the façade was over.

I politely asked him, "So, who are you without all that stuff…the shades, earring and tongue ring?" I could tell by the expression on his face that no one had ever asked him anything like that before.

His next action surprised himself more than it did me. He said, "I am Fire and I don't need things to define who I am." I agreed with him as I slowly removed his movie star shades, then seductively stared at him and held out my hand for his tongue ring.

He sensed the seriousness of the moment and retreated to the bathroom to remove it. Not in a million years did I really think he would give up the tongue ring so quickly. At that moment I knew we were off to a great start. I also knew there would come a time when he would discover that he had met a sanctified closet freak. Yes, I know that's an oxymoron. Obviously, the two words don't go together. But that was part of my own *façade*, as you will discover. And, Fire would soon discover 'Cover' was undercover.

Our relationship grew like most. We talked on the phone constantly and shared weekends together. Sadly though, Fire was a new breed gentleman. He wasn't big on opening doors or seating me first on dinner dates. But, he was big on eating and

.....................

*If you keep your mouth shut, you will stay out of trouble.*

Proverbs 21:23 (NLT)

standing over me to mark his territory. He didn't deviate from his weekly routine after each date – surprisingly, he always took me straight home. Each time, my flesh wanted to invite him to stay. But my spirit was telling me not to extend the invitation. We never pushed the issue; we took each day as it came. Time and time again, he would drive his exhausted self home, while I kept him awake on the phone. His actions showed that he respected me and I appreciated his thoughtfulness.

Often, he'd come over after church on Sunday to visit and eat. I would time his arrival as we talked on the phone. He already knew what I'd cooked and was ready to be treated like a king on his throne. He always greeted me with his famous line, "what's up Cover?", kissed me, washed his hands, and then seated himself at the head of the dinner table. I took pride in learning what he liked and how he wanted it cooked.

However, there came a time when we decided to share more than just food, if you know what I mean. In doing so, I sometimes took on wifely duties like: washing and ironing his clothes, shining his shoes, pulling his ingrown hairs, massaging his body and fixing his weekend breakfast. There was only one problem - we weren't married! Don't get me wrong, he did many things for me too. But the fact still remains, we WEREN'T married!

At the time, that information didn't matter to me because Fire was unique. I wanted to believe he thought the same

...................

*Do not praise yourself; let others do it.*

Proverbs 27:2 (NLT)

about me. I knew his family was crazy about me, but he was hard to read. So, I started asking questions during our quality time.

I could tell he wanted to share some things with me, but I didn't know what. Eventually, he gained enough confidence in me to finally share his intimate secrets. It didn't take much time for me to reciprocate. Each month brought a deeper fondness for sharing.

A few things started happening after that that led me to believe he really trusted me. I don't mean trusted me around men. Because he knew I was the type of women that gave my all to the man I was with. I didn't believe in sharing. I mean, he trusted me with his personal identifiable information; bank account numbers and social security number, etc.

Eventually, his gospel play returned to the road for a few months. And if you do any traveling you know it's hard to handle some business while on the road. So, Fire called. He was frustrated and needed my help to resolve some business on his behalf. Without hesitation, he provided account numbers, social security number and a point of contact. At first, I wondered why he didn't ask his family to assist. Then, I remembered some things he confided in me about them. Based on those unfortunate incidents, my involvement made more sense. So, I handled the business for him.

....................

*Fear of the Lord is the beginning of knowledge; only fools despise wisdom and discipline.*

Proverbs 1:7 (NLT)

Later, he called from another city and I provided an update. He always expressed his gratitude and enlightened me with the drama unfolding in each tour city. All I could do was patiently wait on his return home. I know it may seem like we were living together. But we weren't. We just spent enough time together for me to really miss him.

Each day became longer and longer. My work days seemed extremely hectic when he was out of town. Although I knew his itinerary, it didn't beat him being home. Many days their schedule would only permit them to stay in certain cities for short amounts of time. I became accustomed to his calls just to say, "hello" and "goodnight". I thought that was fine. Even though there came a time when he was on tour and I couldn't tell if I missed him or the intimacy more. As long as he was out of town working, my flesh wasn't tempted to fornicate.

Upon his return, it was routine for us to visit the music store. I tried so hard to fit into "his" world of music by studying "his" craft. I became consumed with knowing the different types of percussion equipment.

Drum sticks and snares continued dancing in my head while my eardrums throbbed into the night. I knew knowledge was power in impressing him. It became imperative that I learn music lingo and acronyms in order to keep up with him. But, there was one major problem — this was HIS world, not mine. I was trying to fit in where I didn't.

In crossing the line and becoming intimate, I noticed a few more things. I'm not 'shamed to say, that he was the only man that allowed me to be myself in the bedroom. I know it sounds crazy, but it's the truth. We were into the same freaky things. It was normal for us to alternate between dominating and surrendering to each other. Whether in a handstand, April shower, sixty-nine, masturbation, using bull rings and the bullet, watching adult movies, we experienced it together. When we played with my toys, we did it together.

He boasted about his reputation for conquering women on his knees. But, he let my school teacher appearance fool him. Because neither one of us were praying when we were on our knees. We were both doing some damage. We didn't want to just watch porn. We duplicated it in the bedroom without any cameras.

We used each other as props and let our inhibitions go. It didn't take him long to determine that he had met his match.

There was *no* place our tongues were scared to explore. No region was off limits from the top of our heads to the soles of our feet. As much as I wanted to hang from the ceiling fan, weight restraints crushed that thought. So, I settled for hanging off the bed railing. If it was erotic or sensual, we probably tried it to the tenth power. I made it my job to keep him weak in the knees, if not comatose before he conquered me. For these reasons, ole folks used to say, "It's not good to sit on someone's bed because you don't know what spirits are on it."

I think I scared Fire one night during one of our erotic sessions. The more we played, the more my mind flashed back to being fondled and raped. My body became limp and tears rolled from my eyes. He didn't know what to do. He kept asking, "What did I do? What did I do"? I assured him 'nothing' and I finally opened up about the two incidents. I explained my logic for suppressing the events and never disclosing it to my parents. He understood because he had hidden a few secrets from his family too. I rested in his arms as tears rolled from the corners of my eyes. Eventually, I fell asleep as the memories dried on my face, but no longer hid in my heart.

I hope it's understood what I mean when I say we were selling our souls to the devil through each novelty item, bags of toys, edible lotions, adult movie, seductive lingerie, bondage item and sex act. You do know that sin enters through your five senses: what you see, feel, hear, taste and smell.

Just the thought of Fire quenched my appetite and I filled his. We weren't scared to teach each other our tricks. In fact, it became a competition to see who could drain the other faster. Isn't it funny that the ONE thing we had in common turned into a competition? I know some of you are saying TMI (too much information).

Really it's not though, because there is a purpose behind sharing this.

You need to know how deep into sexual immorality I had traveled in order to understand my praise today. It makes no sense to tell you half of my testimony. I have to tell you the whole truth; which is the good, bad and ugly. Especially since Fire was trying to educate me on the darker side of sexual immorality.

He told me about hermaphrodites (morphodites/ morpho-dikes), people that had both male and female reproductive organs, and suburban sex parties. He didn't need to attend himself; believers sent him pictures online all the time.

Unfortunately, like some men, he desired to have his fantasy fulfilled. Yes, you guessed it…a ménage tois. That devil is a liar! I wasn't going to cross that bridge. The thought of it turned the pit of my stomach. I knew at that time that our relationship would be on shaky ground when he heard me refuse that idea. However, that didn't stop him from mentioning it from time to time. I was hoping he would come up with another fantasy for me to consider. But he didn't.

It was during that season of our relationship that I became restless and could only sleep a few hours at a time. The rest of the night I tossed and turned; walking the floor became a ritual. My mind started pondering over losing him over that stupid fantasy. Plus, I had become convicted about fornicating. I wrestled between stopping fornication and second guessing my decision to fill his fantasy. Our relationship was on the line.

I didn't think it would take my hair falling out and weight loss for me to come to my senses. Again, I had fallen in love with the wrong man.

Fire and I began arguing more and more. My suppressed anger and hurt from previous relationships started to surface with a vengeance. The self-control I had was now gone. It didn't help that my son became rebellious and disobedient during this time. He pushed my tolerance level to its limit after showing signs of possessing the same sexual demons.

It didn't take long before I began feeling overwhelmed and defeated. This prompted my category 5 hurricane, which reached wind speeds of 155 mph and surges at 18 ft high.

One night in particular, I finally fell asleep without a headache and extra relationship drama. I was fatigued and mentally drained from battling with Fire and my son. My mind slowly started drifting into a comfortably sound sleep. Then I began dreaming.

The dream started out very simple…I was laying on my right side while sleeping on the right side of the bed. All of a sudden out of nowhere I felt something moving under the top sheet. Without waking up, I kicked at it with my left foot. The next thing I remember, a snake appeared and we started wrestling in the bed. In a semi-conscious state of mind, I could feel my body tossing from left to right.

I woke up hyperventilating and terrified. I was exhausted and felt like I had been in a physical fight. More so, I was paranoid because I DON'T LIKE SNAKES of any kind. I jumped up and turned on the light to make sure nothing was in the bed. I felt like a little kid, I even pulled all the covers back to double check. Of course nothing was there.

My mind was playing tricks on me; I kept feeling something crawling on me. And I couldn't stop brushing imaginary crawling things off my gown. Once my pulse rate returned to normal, I got back in the bed. It took a little while before I fell back to sleep. I realized later that this wasn't just a dream…it was a warning!

The next day, Fire came over after church to visit and eat dinner. I told him about my strange dream of wrestling with a snake. I told him that I remembered having a similar dream when I was young. He mentioned that he had a friend who interprets dreams and offered to contact her, which he did. For some strange reason though, when he was dialing her number I became nervous. I'm still trying to figure out if it was due to already knowing what the dream meant or confirmation that my relationship with Fire would be jeopardized.

Fire got Ms. P on the phone and explained that I needed my dream interpreted. I didn't have a problem sharing it with her because we knew of each other, but had not personally met. He passed me the phone, I said, "Hello Ms. P this is Linda." She said, "Hello; explain your dream." The atmosphere in the room changed. Silence fell on both ends of the phone. It took a minute for me to utter a word. Finally, I proceeded to share with her what I shared with him. I also informed her that I'd had a similar dream when I was young. But the Lord didn't reveal the ending in either dream.

When I finished, Ms. P said, "Your dream means you are wrestling with something. You're in bed with a snake; in bed with something trying to hurt you." She asked if I knew what she was talking about. I replied, "Yes, I know...fornication." Then she asked if Fire and I were still sleeping together. I told her that we were and that I had become convicted by it. At that moment, I knew I needed to talk to Fire about abstinence. I was finally ready to stop fornicating...or, so I thought!

In mid 2005, I received a prophetic word from my co-worker, Ketra Wilkerson. By coincidence, we both walked into the ladies room at the same time. At that time I didn't know she was a prophetess, I only knew that she was anointed.

She looked at me and proceeded to tell me that there was some negative energy seeping from my pores. At first I gave her a strange look; then she told me that she could see that something had a stronghold on me. She warned me that if I didn't remove those things from my life, they could *kill* me.

I knew at that time that I was wrestling with a devilish, demonic spirit that was trying to kill me. It wanted to pull me into the pits of hell with my sheets wrapped around me. That day I felt the Lord was tired of messing with me, so he sent a stronger message through Prophetess Wilkerson.

She and I routinely spoke, but I never mentioned that I was wrestling with fornication. Again, it was visible that I had chosen simple pleasures over God's voice. You could tell God wasn't ready to leave me alone though. I let a few days pass, then asked Fire if we could talk. I openly shared my conviction about fornication. I asked if we could abstain from sex and try being celibate. He fought it tooth and nail before saying he couldn't do it cold turkey. So, I made a deal with him to cut back on the sex a little at a time.

The day I had waited for finally arrived...our first day of celibacy. It was also the beginning of Fire's horrible attitude shift. After a few weeks of celibacy, he decided it was better for him not to visit me as much. He couldn't take smelling my body spray and seeing me in certain types of clothing. So, I made adjustments at home in order to please him. But, the atmosphere of my home was still too tempting for him.

His attitude got so bad I couldn't take it anymore. I surrendered to him and we began fornicating again. However, his body didn't feel the same. The Lord had taken the desire and taste for him away. By that time, our relationship was past the boiling point; it had exploded. We both were dissatisfied with each other. We could no longer please each other and both grew tired of the nonsense. Not long after that, our two year relationship dissolved.

Months after our break-up, my mind humbly accepted a few facts. Apparently, we had ignored all the red flags from the first conversation forward. Our compatibility consisted of intense intimacy. Two terrible dating mishaps were revealed in my quiet time. First, we weren't completely healed prior to meeting. Second, we developed a sensual relationship that turned sexual fast.

A lot of people make the same huge mistake in dealing with their sin. They tend to retreat from it and later try to return to the sinfulness. This can lead to continuous thoughts of unrighteousness. Or, in simple terms, stagnation. And that is what happened to me. I became convinced Fire and I could work things out if he would communicate with me. He didn't see it like that though. He cut off all communication and later changed his phone number. Even though it hurt, I accepted his decision, repented of my sins and took a vow of celibacy. At that moment I became yoked with God. I now desired what He desired for me.

Sadly, something else was revealed during that time as well. Fornication and sex-toys had turned me out and blinded me from the truth. And *my* truth became a lie. I played with temptation and got burned. I chose to self-medicate on sin. Almost everything I thought I knew about love, intimacy and a relationship were wrong. At the rate I was going, it would've been the *death* of me.

How many of you know that when you're not taught right or the street is your teacher, bad habits are picked up? Well, that's what happened to me. I "picked up" some bad information and habits from the streets and other sources.

The Lord had no other choice. He had to empty me of the lies in order to fill me with His truth. His word IS the truth. He replaced my lies -- lust was love, each relationship was a set up for a future, my knowledge was filling me instead of killing me, pain wasn't self induced, fornication and sex-toys were my God -- with His word -- God is love, -- I'm a jealous God and will have no other God before me, delight yourself in me, and I will give you the desires of your heart and out of the heart flows the issues of life. Things were finally becoming clear for a change.

Do you see similarities in your life and my testimony? If we have some things in common, God is faithful and just. He forgives us of our sins and moves us toward our purpose. Let's walk together.

Bottom line, I chose not to listen to the Lord because I didn't want to be lonely. I was disobedient and had a phobia about being alone. I wasn't used to *not* being with a man or in a relationship. And I enjoyed what I was doing.

A dear friend once told me that I was in love with being in love. At first I told him he was wrong, and then I pondered over his words. He was right!

I felt needed and wanted when I was involved in a relationship, whether my partner was committed to me or not.

Let me keep it real, I desired the company of a man. So, like some women and men, I settled for relationships that weren't sanctioned by my Heavenly Father. This way of thinking assisted me in defiling the name of the Lord by engaging in sexual immorality.

It wasn't until I started hearing and *receiving* the voice of God in my spirit that my life started to take on a different shape. See, I heard a voice, but was scared to heed what the voice told me, due to loving the wrong man.

There are no big initials behind my name. I'm not a doctor, therapist, prophet, minister, theologian or seminary student. I'm an ordinary single mom of a young man who has been through many storms, trials and tribulations and didn't learn from the lessons.

As a result, the Lord sent me through more storms and trials before the light went off. By the time my light went off, I was in my late 30's. Yes, I know you're asking, "What took so long?" Well, let me answer that in one word... DISOBEDIENCE. I wanted to do things my way because it was the only way I knew. Besides, that is what people do when they straddle the fence between carnality and spirituality.

Even though there are many reasons we need to return to the basics, I wasn't surprised when the Lord birth into my spirit that *I* must return to the basics with regards to learning the definition of words. In doing so, I would understand the words of my sin in order to deter me from the action. In order for me to understand where he was leading me, I first had to understand the definition of the words used to describe my disobedience. You may have to do the same thing. I believe many of us are guilty of repeating words, phrases and clichés that we heard someone use. Do like I did, go to the bookstore, buy a bible dictionary and other study tools that will enable you to better understand the word of God through word study.

Shortly after that, the Holy Spirit confirmed (through a sermon of our associate minister, Rev. Kelly) that sometimes we must do a word study to elevate our understanding of the words we use. This is done because one word may lead us to another word that needs to be defined for clarity. The first words given to me to define was:

*Defiled:* To make foul, dirty, or unclean; to violate the chastity; to desecrate; to sully as a person's reputation.

*Chastity:* The state or quality of being chaste.

*Chaste:* Refraining from unsanctioned sexual activity, celibate, decent and modest.

In now understanding the meaning of these words, it was clear that I had defiled the name of Jesus the Christ. Not just with my thoughts, but with all five of my senses.

Remember early in the book I explained that I heard *a voice* speaking to me, but I didn't recognize it as being His voice. Oh yes, I went to church every Sunday (sometimes 2-3 times), sang in the choir and later became a reluctant

. . . . . . . . . . . . . . . . . . . .

*Each heart knows its own bitterness, and no one else can fully
share its joy.*

Proverbs 14:10 (NLT)

deaconess…and still didn't recognize His voice. I was in church, but church wasn't in me.

I made an unconscious decision not to listen to His Godly wisdom trying to spare me from many years of defiled relationships not sanctioned by Him.

Thank God for His forgiving power. He gave me not a second chance, but another, and another, and another chance to truly get lined up with His will for my life. He is so awesome; I cannot thank him enough! Now, it's time to get back to the basics and understand who we are in Christ Jesus.

....................

*My sheep hear My voice, and I know them, and they follow Me. And I give them eternal life, and they shall never perish; neither shall anyone snatch them out of my hand. My Father, who has given them to Me, is greater than all; and no one is able to snatch them out of My Father's hand. I and My Father are one.*

John 10:27-30 (NKJV)

# Part Two

## Back 2 Basics

Photo: Linda D. Lee

# 5

# *"Virtuous" Defined*

**Proverbs 31:10 KJV: Who can find a virtuous woman? For her price is far above rubies.** Depending on your bible translation it may read: *Who can find a virtuous wife?* So, I'm going to expound on this verse from a woman's perspective because "wife" in this verse, is also interpreted to mean "woman".

Many women desire to be a *virtuous* woman, but don't know what that means. A virtuous woman is a lady that conducts herself with class and eloquence. She is graceful and poised. She is strong, yet submissive. She is intelligent, empowering and lives a righteous life.

Virtuous means: (1) conforming to moral and ethical principles (2) chaste. Chaste is defined as: refraining from unsanctioned sexual activity. Random House Webster's Dictionary. A virtuous <u>wife</u> knows her duty is to her husband and family. And there are activities she is authorized to perform according to the word. She is a caregiver to her children. As such, she must care for the intimate needs of her husband.

They cannot deprive one another, except with consent for a time. See 1 Corinthians 7:5 NLT.

While an <u>unmarried</u> virtuous woman knows her duty is to the Lord. She should be busy doing ministry work and delighting herself in Him. Therefore, if the Lord has not joined you in marriage, you should consider celibacy and practice abstinence. Also, He doesn't recognize "shacking", also known as "living together." It's an unrighteous act that contradicts your virtuous testimony.

**Proverbs continues with Verse 15: She riseth also while it is yet night, and giveth meat to her household, and a portion to her maidens.** This verse demonstrates that she cooked and cared for the nutritional needs of her family and others. She got up early to prepare, provide and pray for the food they were about to receive. This demonstrates her unselfishness.

She thought about others first and herself last. She produced from the herbs and seeds of the ground. But, it was an honor to present the prepared meat; the fruit of her labor. She was compassionate about her family and nutrition. Most importantly, she shared a portion of the meal with others. This expresses a giving spirit and consideration for others. And in order to have a giving spirit, you must have the spirit of God in you.

NOTE: If you are to regain your virtuous qualities, you must also transform your eating habits. This includes your portions and seasoning. Yes, I know granny — cooked ham hocks, pig feet, chitterlings and seasoned meats with salt jowl is what you're used to. But, if you rework your diet it could reduce your cholesterol, fat, sodium or sugar intake. Utilize your funds and purchase a healthy cooking guide. With all the healthy cooking aids available, it doesn't make sense to clog your arteries with fatty substances.

**Verse 17: She girdeth her loins with strength, and strengtheneth her arms. This verse speaks to her being healthy and wise. She had to exercise and maintain balance in her life.**

NOTE: Keep your annual check-up and dental appointments. Diabetes, heart disease, high blood pressure and stroke indicators are mainly detected during scheduled visits. Some diseases are noticed during dental exams. HIV/AIDS won't have a chance if more people practice celibacy and abstinence. Take care of your hygiene and hair care. Get off the couch and exercise 2-3 times a week. Start with a 30 minute walk.

**Verse 24: She maketh fine linen, and selleth it; and delivereth girdles unto the merchant. She was an entrepreneur, seamstress and business woman. She was not scared to work.**

NOTE: Stop sitting around waiting on a window of opportunity or hand out. God gives us opportunities every day. He is waiting on you to take it and work while it is yet day. Learn how to sew or take up a hobby.

**Verse 25: Strength and honour are her clothing; and she shall rejoice in time to come. She took pride in her appearance and she praised God for the blessing.**

NOTE: Don't dishonor God by dressing unrighteous, enticing, alluring or even provocative. Cover up around your sons and daughters as a sign of respect to them and yourself. Remember your G-strings, thongs or boy-shorts are UNDERwear, not OUTERwear. These comments aren't necessarily for babes in Christ. God will change the way they dress. But you seasoned saints KNOW BETTER!

Let me remind you, God holds you accountable for the things you know. Check your motive for what you are wearing. If your motive isn't right, I need you to stop right here and jump to the section *A Hot Mess*. Then return to this section later.

Now, back to my suggestions. Test your clothes against sunlight or room light. Hold it up to the light or put on your dress or skirt and bend over and touch your toes. Can you see thru it? If so, it doesn't pass the light test and you need to put on a slip. Virtuous doesn't equal visible. You shouldn't want someone seeing thru your articles of clothing, especially at church.

Further, while attending church, use a lap cover (oversized square scarf) in case your skirt is too short while seated. If your blouse shows too much cleavage, use a safety pin to close the opening.

Bottom line, if the outfit doesn't glorify God, throw it away. **Don't give it away...throw it away.** Repeat and rehearse basic manners and church etiquette. Remember you attend church to receive a word from God, not draw attention away from the word. Keep in mind your daughter, granddaughter or niece is watching you. They may mimic what they see you do.

**Verse 26: She openeth her mouth with wisdom; and in her tongue is the law of kindness.** She was conscious of the words coming out of her mouth. She spoke words of encouragement that lifted your spirit. She wasn't scared to share her knowledge with others. She spoke pleasant, tender words every time she opened her mouth. She made a rule (law) to only speak kindness. She had a set principle of touching words that ministered to you. She dominated the conversation with wisdom. Every time she opened her mouth she spoke with sweet authority.

NOTE: If you don't have anything good to say, don't say ANYTHING at all. Take a 30 day tongue fast challenge and work on these tongues: Lying, Manipulating, Argumentativeness, Boasting, Gossiping, Belittling, Intimidating, Rudeness, Cursing and Complaining. If you have a lying tongue work on it daily. For the Lord detests a lying tongue. Proverbs 6:17b. Challenge yourself daily. Don't be discouraged; continue to strive at becoming a virtuous woman.

. . . . . . . . . . . . . . . . . . ..

*Pleasant words are like a honey comb, Sweetness to the soul and health to the bones.*

Proverbs 16:24 (NKJV)

# 6

# Traits of a Godly Man — Before He Sinned

In order to understand *Godly*, I studied the historical meaning of the word. In doing so, the Holy Spirit revealed this information:

*Godly: (Heb., Hasid) (Gk., eusebes)
(1) Old Testament definition - those who have received and responded to God's grace; (2) New Testament definition — those whose faith in God is expressed by obedience.

Man:  (1) An adult male person.

(2) The human race; humankind.

*Richard's Bible Dictionary.*

I returned to the beginning of the Bible in order to introduce the traits of a Godly man – before he sinned. We all know the history of creation began in Genesis 1: 1-2 (NKJV) with,

*"In the beginning God created the heavens and the earth. The earth was without form, and void; and darkness was on the face of the deep. And the Spirit of God was hovering over the face of the waters."* These scriptures help you see God's majestic power. His creations didn't stop there.

I want to draw your attention to verse 27 of the same chapter, which reads, "So God created man in His image; in the image of God He created him; male and female He created them." You should rejoice in knowing God created us in His image. Not your earthly father, grandfather or uncle, but His image. Chapter 2 verse 7 shows the magnitude of his tender love for us when He formed man from of the dust of the ground, and breathed into his nostrils the breath of life; and man became a living being.

Let me expound...**In his image:** We were created in the image of God. And God is love and his image (likeness) is humbling. According to *Webster's Dictionary*, "Humbling" is defined as, not proud or arrogant; and respectful; and to lower in pride. His image represents purity, holiness and righteousness.

**Formed from the dust:** He shaped us into distinction. He organized and arranged our silhouette. He specifically designed us with intricate unique details. He took matter in fine dry particles from the ground and formed us.

**Breathed into his nostrils life:** He inhaled and exhaled a whisper of air into the two external openings of the nose. That shows his closeness, tenderness and affection to us. He drew in (inhaled) and released (exhaled) a soft mixture of nitrogen, oxygen, and minute amounts of other gases that surround the earth, into his nostrils.

## BOTTOM LINE

A Godly man exemplifies:

(1) Godly love at all times; (2) A holy relationship with God; (3) Purity and righteousness; (4) An understanding of his purpose; (5) The creator daily. (6) The spirit of God, which is the mind of God.

Question: How many traits do you possess?

. . . . . . . . . . . . . . . . . .

*Source: Richard's Complete Bible Dictionary*

# 7

## Healing Beyond the Past

You can't be an effective example to someone else if your internal spirit still has a 10 year old bandage on the wound. Let me help this statement to live with this hypothetical example:

Picture yourself with a bandage on a sore. The sore has been on your arm for a month. For two weeks puss and blood has been seeping from the sore. Everyone around you insists that you need to go to the doctor. Especially, since it hasn't healed. You decide the sore doesn't look that bad, even though it is turning green. I'm not a rocket scientist, but even I know any sore that turns green is probably infected and requires immediate doctor's attention.

Again, being the stubborn one, you insist the sore is ok. Each day the coloration in your arm looks darker and darker. The sore has turned into an ugly wound. Then, one day when your arm feels numb you decide to rush to the emergency room. Upon arriving at the emergency room in a panic, the receptionist takes one look at your arm, and then urgently calls for the doctor. The doctor asks why you waited to come in with such a bad infection on your arm. All you can say is, "I thought I could handle it by myself." The doctor informs you that if you had let a doctor attend to your sore early, gangrene wouldn't have set into your blood. Now, there is a chance you may lose your arm because you didn't allow a doctor to help you sooner. Hearing those strong words were a wake-up call for you.

Well, that is what the Lord has been saying to us from the very beginning, he is our doctor, surgeon, healer and redeemer, all in one. He will heal each and every one of our wounds. He has enough power to mend any broken pieces while we cry out to him. The main difference between us playing the doctor and him BEING the doctor is… he won't just place a bandage on your wound. He will guide you into recovery, cover your scar with his blood, allow his almighty power to dispense medicine into your wound, make the scar become a scab and fall off your arm with *one exhale*. He doesn't need *our* help to heal people; we need *His* help to heal ourselves, then others. Too many times the Lord sends us signals, signs, confirmation, revelations and other storms to show us how to stop living in the flesh. Most of these times, our own disobedience is our stumbling block toward the purpose God has for us. I allowed over 30 years of ignoring the Lords voice, of which, 15 years were a pity party, to stifle my spiritual growth.

. . . . . . . . . . . . . . . . . . .

*The fear of the Lord prolongs days, but the years of the wicked will be shortened.*

Proverbs 10:27 (NKJV)

Glory, Hallelujah! I was finally ready to exchange my battle scars with a weapon of praise. I confessed my sinful ways and asked for God's forgiveness. I started fighting my flesh in the spirit. Immediately, I took my hands off the situation and:

- Let God take control over my mind.
- Developed a rightful relationship with Him.
- Actively pulled down my own stronghold.
- Allowed God to remove (obstacles) people, places and things from my life.
- De-cluttered or detached from anything linked to my past. This included materialistic items, souvenirs, clothes and jewelry. If it was not conducive to my spiritual growth, it was eliminated or given away.

Remember, when a mental storm or temptation comes:

1. Find a quiet place to retreat.
2. Lay prostrate before God.
3. Speak and cry out to Him.
4. Stand still and listen for HIS voice daily.

Storms are not accidents. They are predestined incidents in time. According to *Webster's Dictionary*, "Incidents" are occurrences or events. They could be minor or lead to serious

..................

*Deal with your past; don't let it deal with you. Move On!*

consequences. So, trust God and praise Him in your storm. Praise Him for the minor or major circumstance HE allowed into your life. Those incidents are a test of your faith. And we all know it is written, *"faith without works is dead."* James 2:20. Faith also keeps you rooted despite the changes around you. It allows you to understand that your success is based on its existence. Most importantly, it operates as an entity through which to handle your past, present and future adversities. We need a right now faith that moves you from the nature realm to a spiritual realm of exercising your faith. Also, keep in mind your opposition will not move until you learn how to obey God's word. Never feel alone because faith is working on your behalf and grace and mercy are following you. Now, that's enough to make you shout!

. . . . . . . . . . . . . . . . . .

*Let us therefore make every effort to do what leads to peace and to mutual edification.*

Romans 14:19 (NIV)

# 8

# *Internal Healing and Deliverance*

This word was given to me for the purpose of helping *people* heal and be delivered, not just women. Ideally, most people think only women need to heal. This is where some people make a huge mistake in their thought pattern. Men have feelings and hurt similar to women. The way they react and respond to their hurt may be different, but they can be emotionally devastated too. Men are good at maintaining a brave face while their heart is aching inside. If you have been hurt in any capacity, my testimony should assist you in your healing process.

God gives us choices. The decisions we make in life are up to us. He wants us to establish a right relationship with Him. Increase your quality time with God. By now you should love The Master enough to become more involved or more committed to his will and way. He is our source for spiritual nutrition to our souls. We should thank him with:

- Contagious generosity.
- Consistent praise and worship.
- Giving to others and witnessing.
  (This is a form of washing others' feet like Jesus did his disciples.)

Now, I will wash your feet by introducing additional steps to my healing journey. You can't truly understand your purpose until you, (1) Recognize you have a problem; (2) Verbally acknowledge the problem; (3) Seek resolution of the problem.

In order for God to elevate you, events have to happen his way. You must go through His process, His way, not yours. He will separate you from people that aren't a part of your growth. You may feel it's not fair, or that it's a drastic move to get your attention. Always remember that it's part of the purging process and your spiritual makeover.

Most healing processes are five to eight stages. You will experience these stages in no particular order:

- **Shock** – you don't know or understand what just happened.
- **Numbness** – you're surprised you missed the signs or let it happen to you again.
- **Denial** – you can't believe it happened to you or you didn't do anything wrong for it to happen.

- **Fear** – you won't be able to trust again and become suspicious of everyone.

- **Depression** – you become more insecure or reclusive. Darkness and unrighteous behavior becomes your friend.

- **Anger** – resentment builds because they moved on with their life or they become involved in another relationship.

- **Forgiveness** – you understand your worth, (who you are in Christ) by letting the past go.

- **Acceptance** – you finally receive that past events were God's predestined will.

It doesn't matter which stage you're in right now. Your obedience to God can make the stage longer or shorter. If you have a <u>desire</u> to be delivered from any or all of your issues, you must make the first step by opening up your mouth and speaking it into existence. I can't state that enough.

Your **heart** has to turn from sin daily. People don't understand how important heart health is as a part of - their recovery from sin. *For out of the **heart** flows the issues of life.* Proverbs 4:23 NKJV. When your heart isn't right, neither are your actions.

God reminds us, *"If your right eye causes you to sin (offends you), pluck it out and **cast it from you**; for it is more profitable for you that one of your members perish, than for your whole body to be cast into hell. And if your right hand causes you to sin, cut it off and **cast it from you**; for it is* *more profitable for you that one of your members perish, than for your whole body to be cast into hell."* Matthew 5: 29-30 NKJV.

Christ speaks figuratively. He wants you to understand this from a spiritual perspective. He doesn't want you to mutilate your body by physically cutting your eyes or hand. He wants you to take the burning desire *for the sin* out of your **heart** and you won't have lust in your eyes.

When I was carnal minded, sin entered through my five senses. However, God has been perfecting me since that time. My five senses are now occupied by righteousness, under the direction of the Holy Spirit. Therefore, I moved from carnality to spirituality. Now, my senses are mature. I now understand that the lamp of my body is my eyes. See Matthew 6:22a NKJV. If my eye is good, my whole body will be full of *light*. This means, I moved from the darkness into His marvelous *light*. I have stepped into another dimension under God's mighty hand.

Grace and mercy continued following me like the children being lead out of Egypt with God in a cloud. Therefore, my ears were open to receiving and understanding His will for my life. The things I touched and tasted were no longer tainted. It took many years, but I finally fell in love with the right man. I started hiding His word in my heart so I might not sin against Him. See Psalms 119: 1 NKJV.

Your spiritual senses can also be opened, your vision can be clear, and righteous desires can flow from your **heart**. This is a major step in your deliverance process. Aren't you ready to walk in the light and see things clearly? Just say,

"Lord I surrender to *your* will." Yes, it is that easy. It is time to walk away from your past into your predestined purpose. Though everybody's deliverance process will be different, surrendering to God's will is common.

. . . . . . . . . . . . . . . . . . .

*Finally, brethren, whatsoever things are true, whatsoever things are honest, whatsoever things are just, whatsoever things are pure, whatsoever things are lovely, whatsoever things are of good report; if there be any virtue, and if there be any praise, think on these things. Those things, which ye have both learned, and received, and heard, and seen in me, do: and the God of peace shall be with you.*

Philippians 4:8 (KJV)

*Covered*

Part Three

# Advice

# Guide

# 9

# The End Result

I could feel my continued healing in a chain of events that started in late 2008. I knew something major was coming because everything around me became silent. People were unavailable for my calls, but reached me constantly at work with a word from the Lord.

In October 2008, Pastor Willis was in revival at Mount Rose Church for three nights. One night he preached an awesome word, *Your Ticket Out of the Wilderness.* This was my break-through service. It was the first time I saw the Glory of the Lord visually fall on the Mount. The best way I can describe it is like this: A haze of light came over the pulpit and spread the width of a section of pews. The soft light became a little brighter and lasted a few minutes. It looked like there was an extra light over the pulpit. It also seemed a little cooler in the sanctuary. And I could see small particles falling like snow; but, it never hit the ground. They evaporated at the point, where the haze met the preachers shadow in the pulpit. I couldn't take my eyes off the particles. I felt like God was raining down grace and mercy on Mount Rose to regenerate His children.

My soul was ready to receive the message from the Lord. So, I made my way to the altar for prayer. I didn't know at that time that Bishop was going to lay hands on us during the prayer. That encounter with God was the first time I was slain in the spirit. I had witnessed it before, but never experienced it myself. I now understand why. He was perfecting me spiritually in order to handle where he was taking me on my journey.

The Lord confirmed in that service my departure from Grace Tabernacle Missionary Baptist Church under Pastor Brackins and Lady Brackins. And the power of the Holy Spirit united me with Mount Rose Church under the anointed Bishop Jeffery Thomas, Sr. All of which play an intricate part in my spiritual growth.

When Bishop kicked the New Year off with, *Taking Up What's Been Keeping You Down,* I knew God was going to move on my behalf in 2009. Every message he preached or taught shaped me. A few sermons directly impacted my journey: March 29, *The Weariness in Well Doing;* April 29, *A New Creature and Vision Brings Victory;* May 3, *Fight the Flesh in the Spirit;* June 14, *Driven by the Spirit;* June 21, *Lightening Your Load;* and June 28, *Are You Really Ready?*

But on Sunday, June 28, during 7 o'clock service, the anointing fell on Mount Rose when he preached, *Saints In The Wrong Place.* In the middle of the service, God gave him this prophetic word for the church. He instructed us to read 1 Kings 19:1-13 for 40 days. He spoke of God showing up after

the wind, earthquake, fire and 40 days in the wilderness…
in a small voice. I knew that was a word for me, so I started
reading the scripture the next day and listened for His voice
regarding this book. The following Saturday was July 4th I was
scheduled to work the prayer lines for our church television
broadcast, *Count It All Joy*. In the middle of the broadcast,
the atmosphere shifted and Bishop declared…**not many days
hence.** Based on my prayer request, I knew that was another
word for me to brace myself for what was coming. God was
getting ready to move!

Well, Friday morning July 10, Sis. Gail called me at work
with another prophetic word from the Lord. She said, *"God
is trying to talk to you. You are still too busy. You need to be
still and find a place of solitude…I see 3 days."* She didn't
know that prior to her call I was contemplating moving up my
scheduled vacation in preparation for surgery.

After that message from God, my spirit began to move.
I pushed my vacation up, adjusted my work schedule and
cleared my desk off to begin my vacation that evening. Once I
arrived home, I began searching in the phone book for a place
of solitude. It was 3 a.m. Saturday, July 11th when I located
the perfect refuge. The location would allow me to still attend
church, while spending time with God. I reserved a room for
three days and checked in later that afternoon.

The first night I humbled myself, lied prostrate before
God prayed and cried for direction for the ending of the book.
He didn't answer me and I didn't work on the book at all that
night. Sunday morning, I rose and read 1 Kings Chapter 19
before departing for church.

During the service, the power of the Holy Spirit moved Bishop into the prophetic. He declared: *"God is going to move* ***early in the morning***. *You got to get up early before the sun rises. Start your prayer time early. This confirms God is going to make an early morning move in your life. Before the sun rises in the morning, your situation is worked out."* I believed the prophet and understood that my time was drawing near due to the magnitude of the message…from **not many days hence** to **early in the morning,** I knew.

My anxiety level was building. I could see God's awesome power move right before my eyes each Sunday. The church body was no longer in an anointed atmosphere. It felt like we had reached the second or third heaven, when the Glory of the Lord showed up. The church turned our altar into the Jerusalem Wailing Wall. Praise and worship had elevated to a ridiculous level as the Holy Ghost came upon our members. Most of us left church still drunk under the anointing. It is something I will never forget!

I returned to my suite to eat something before 7 o'clock service. I kept replaying the prophetic word from the service over and over in my head. In the meantime, anticipation engulfed me as the 7 o'clock hour drew- near.

I couldn't wait to receive another message from the Lord through Bishop. However, the hour at hand came and went quickly with more food for my soul. Again, I returned to my suite to retire for the evening. While sitting on the couch in a quiet room, God gave me some directions for the book. I followed them and wrote in long hand until my writing was blurry. It was late, so I moved slowly to the business center and typed what He had given me.

Monday, July 13 arrived and my time of serenity with God was almost over. I woke up around 4 a.m. to read 1 Kings Chapter 19 prior to returning to bed, due to my late check-out request. I returned home later that evening and used that whole week to write and type what God gave me. However, He still didn't provide directions for the conclusion of the book.

We all know God moves in mysterious ways. Well, he moved quickly on Sunday, July 19 and woke me from a sound sleep. I moved to my manuscript on the dinner table to fill in some missing pieces. The more I wrote, the more I found myself confessing. I cried to the Lord again to help me complete the book. An hour later, He allowed me to return to bed and fall fast asleep.

Around 8 o'clock a.m. He woke me again. I could hear a whisper of the song Amazing Grace playing in my ear. After the first stanza I kept hearing THE END, THE END. I shook my head and said, THE END... that isn't part of the song. I jumped out of the bed and shouted THE END. I knew God was saying END the book. Finally, he had given me his seal of approval. It was no accident that this news came the Sunday prior to my 44th birthday. What a birthday gift! I rejoiced and cried in knowing the Holy Spirit had led me out of the wilderness after more than 30 years.

As for the men of my past... (*I know you're wondering what Mitch disclosed after our divorce). Well, Mitch shared his story of being molested by a male family member when he was young. He hid his confused state- of- mind from everyone for years. In the back of his mind, he felt getting married would prove he was all man. Unfortunately, it did not. Being molested only planted a seed into his decision to engage in homosexuality. I thank God he was eventually delivered from that lifestyle. Sadly, it came with a price. He died peacefully the evening of November 2, 2009. As gratitude for our friendship, God allowed him to drop a white silk rose from heaven at my feet the day before the funeral. I knew this meant, "It is finished;" I had loved him as a friend all the way to the end, fulfilling the scripture.*

*Secret Fire, on the other hand, married within a year of our break up. And based on our last conversation, I conclude that he's still wrestling with sexual demons.*

# 10

# Who's Touching Your Children?

In 2005, I heard a sermon that mentioned that we need to get back to the basics in teaching our children. That pastor emphasized that we, as a church body, need to get back to the basics in areas like: raising our children, chastising, reciprocating good manners, studying God's word and feeding our temple with more spiritual food. The message struck a chord in me because I agreed with him 100%. Bits and pieces of the sermon have lingered in my spirit over the years.

These questions started to unfold in my mind:

* **Q.** What happened to teaching our children to say, "yes ma'am" and "no sir?"

  **A.** Those manners died when prayer was taken out of schools. Plus, parents stopped enforcing it.

- **Q.** What happened to teaching them to say their prayers at night?

  **A.** Parents became workaholics and got lazy.

- **Q.** What happened to "spare the rod, spoil the child?"

  **A.** Tougher laws and dealing with Child Protective Services frightened some parents from having authority over their children.

- **Q.** Who is teaching abstinence, purity, celibacy or how to remain a virgin?

  **A.** This one is too easy...Not many parents are teaching abstinence, purity, celibacy or virginology. (Yes, I made that word up.) However, the streets are teaching our children how NOT to remain a virgin. Everywhere you turn, something sexual is being displayed, sold or mentioned for profit. We now live in a sex- crazed world that is pimping our kids left and right.

- **Q.** Why do children invite themselves into grown folks' conversations?

  **A.** Parents allow it.

- **Q.** Why do children leave home improperly dressed for school or church?

  **A.** Parents allow it. They have become lazy, unconcerned and want the world to help raise their children. Plus, the children see their parent scantily dressed and mimic the parent.

- **Q.** Why do children leave home wearing head scarves, house shoes, stocking caps, do-rags, hair rollers, body piercings or sagging pants, and enter stores or church?

  **A.** Because they mimic their parents! Children do what they see, hear and WITNESS their parents doing. It is obvious that parents have either given up on discipline or they really do not care anymore.

- **Q.** What happened to women combing their daughters' hair the night before church?

  **A.** Again, they have become lazy and easily distracted by other priorities. You see the fruits of their laziness when they walk in church with a **fresh** salon hair do. However, their children's appearance is less than desirable. Nothing upsets me more than seeing a mother looking like a million dollars while her kids reek the scents of poverty. Meaning, you can smell their sweat, dirty clothes or musty feet with each move they make. What a disgrace to your child/children.

- **Q.** What happened to fathers getting their sons' hair cut for the following week?

  **A.** They too became lazy! Seasonal sports seem more important than ensuring that their sons look presentable.

- **Q.** What happened to parents making sure the children have an offering for church?

  **A.** If you spent it Saturday night, you cannot give it on Sunday. Or, if you have it and will not give it, you are still robbing God. Please know your child/ children are watching your every move.

- **Q.** What happened to teenagers having a curfew?

  **A.** Some parents want their children to stay in the streets so they don't have to deal with them. That is why the streets raise so many of our children.

- **Q.** What happened to teenagers babysitting, cutting yards and doing errands for allowance?

  **A.** Parents don't want to teach responsibility. Unfortunately, it appears easier to unjustly reward children with material things, rather than TEACH THEM to work for what they want. This generation is spoiled by their parents, not by society. We're supposed to be training the next generation to be lenders, not borrowers. In doing so, they must know how to be self sufficient. All working age young ladies and men need a JOB if they live under your roof. So, stop accepting excuses as to why they can't find employment. Equip them to understand they need income to meet any future needs. Most importantly, the bible says if a man doesn't work he doesn't eat.

Keep in mind that the age and maturity level of your child may be different. Teach in stages aligned with their age. Example 1: Help them open a bank account and limit what <u>you</u> deposit in it. Periodically check to see how much <u>they</u> have invested in themselves. Example 2: Take them to find a job, but don't fill out the application for them. Example 3: Teach them to cut the grass, but don't pick the grass up afterwards. Have them clean up behind themselves. Teach them not to blow it into the street, that's lazy and doesn't exemplify a spirit of excellence. Example 4: If you have college age students, pay their tuition and make them buy their own books or supplies. (I even have my son contributing to the car insurance.) Example 5: Take them to get a cell phone with the understanding that they need to pay the bill, not you.

All of these things assist in teaching them responsibility and helps you get your house in order.

- **Q.** What happened to parents teaching their children about life, or the 'birds and bees?'

  **A.** It is hard to teach them when no one taught you. It is hard to teach them when you're involved in perverted actions. It is hard to teach them when you need to return to the basics. Start at Genesis 1: 1 and rediscover Adam and Eve before they sinned.

- **Q.** What happened to parents knowing where their children are and what they're doing?

  **A.** Some parents have become unconcerned. Nowadays, people are asking the children WHERE ARE YOUR PARENTS? I see more and more children telling their parents what they're not going to do instead of the other way around. What a shame!

- **Q.** Why do parents drop their children off at church like it is a free babysitting service?

103

**A.** Because they are lazy and lack parenting skills. I can't recall a time when I had a choice to attend church or not. Nor can I remember a time as a child when my parents dropped us off at church and picked us up later. Forsaking the assembly shouldn't be an option for any household. Parents, it's time you wake up and regain authority over your household. Just like your kids need to be working in church, you do too. It's not an option. It's an opportunity and honor to serve God using our gifts and talents.

- **Q.** What happened to parenting skills?

  **A.** Some parents have skills. However, due to immaturity, they play the guilt card to manipulate their own parents or grandparents into raising their own children._

- **Q.** Why have parents stopped introducing God to their children?

  **A.** Because they're not in fellowship with Him themselves. But God is waiting on you to return to him. His arms are wide open, ready to receive you again. Don't delay; tomorrow isn't promised.

- **Q.** HAVE YOU BECOME A SCARY PARENT? Well…have you?

  **A.** Only you can answer that question!

The answer to some of the other questions is very simple. **Some** parents haven't just become scary parents. They have become lazy and unconcerned about their child/children's future. The other answer is: YOU allow your child/children to behave the way they do. To take this a step further, your child/children imitate you. Have you ever heard the saying, "The apple doesn't fall far from the tree?" Well, children are doing some of what they see adults do or say. So, please stop blaming the schools, teachers and other children for the things you should have control over: <u>YOUR</u> HOUSEHOLD AND <u>YOUR</u> KIDS.

Proverbs 22: 6 instructs <u>you</u> to train up a child in the way he should go, and when he is old, he will not depart from it. So, can someone please tell me why some parents stopped training and teaching their children in the way they should go? Let me help you answer this one. I believe some parents stopped trying to train their children because it's a hard job.

As a result of that decision, children stopped feeling that they have to obey adults. **We need to return to the ways we were taught generations ago by our grandparents and ancestors.** It truly does take a village to raise a child. I remember when I was young; there was no excuse I could give my parents or grandparents to not attend church, unless you were sick, of course. It was mandatory that we participated in different ministries. If I even looked like I did not want to do as I was told, one of the elders in the church gave you that *look*. Some of you know what I'm referring too. The *look* seemed to silence the room without one word being spoken.

My mother didn't even have to get up from the church pew for me to know she meant business. When that look didn't work, anyone with a switch off the church tree would do. Or,

I knew when I got home I would get it. Why have we gotten so dignified in church today that we hesitate to discipline our children publicly or privately?

It appears the youth of today are running rampant without supervision. This generation of youth lacks nurturing from adults. It does not matter if the child/children are yours or not. It is our job as parents to deposit substance into our children. Stop relinquishing your parental authority to other entities and parents. Your children are *your* children. They fall under YOUR authority. Even though it does take a village to raise today's youth. That ole folks saying implies that a group of believers will be working together for a common goal. It doesn't imply that you trade your parental responsibility, down to not having or using it. I am so tired of seeing parents dump their children on grandparents or great grandparents, because they no longer want the responsibility that came from their intimate action.

Grandparents and great grandparents have raised their children. Now they want to retire, nurture and provide wisdom to the next generation. They don't necessarily want to start over rearing the next generation from lazy, dysfunctional parents. There comes a time when you must cut the apron string before your strength is drained. Let me remind you of what a parent is.

*Webster's Dictionary* defines 'parent' as (1) a father or mother; (2) a source, origin, or cause; (3) any organism that produces another. We must remind the New Breed Parent that children are a gift from God. Why do you think Hannah, Rachel, Sarah and Elizabeth cried a bitter plea to God for a child? They knew a barren woman was perceived to be cursed. And a barren womb is never satisfied. Proverbs 30:16. Today our Lord and saviour Jesus the Christ has blessed us with children as a gift, and we still seem ungrateful. What is wrong with that picture? I submit if adults don't desire parental responsibility, then greater precautions need to be taken in the future…abstinence! This alone is the reason we need to return to the basics in teaching our children to abstain from sexual activities and live a celibate life until marriage. Touch them with God's word.

**Bottom line:** Some husbands need to <u>stand up</u> and re-gain authority over their household. Some wives need to cover up, sit down and <u>submit</u> to authority over their household. Some children need to <u>surrender</u> and step back into their rightful position under the authority over the household. Unmarried women and men need to be working in ministry. If you are an unmarried, take authority over your house while working for the Lord. And everybody needs to consult with the bible for instructions on how to raise your child(ren).

# 11

## How to be Comfortable In Your Singleness

What If There Was
A New Way To Approve Your Mate?

*(In the form of a Credit Application)*

| Name | Last | | First | Middle | | |
|---|---|---|---|---|---|---|
| Address: | | | | | | |
| | Address | | City | | State | Zip |
| Telephone: | Home # | Work# | | Cell# | | |
| Date of Birth: | | Age | | SS# | | |
| Weight | | Height | | | | |
| Ethnicity: (check) | Black | Hispanic | White | Other | | |

Do you live with any of the following: (circle)

| Grandpa | Parents | Mother | Father | Girlfriend | Baby Mama | Alone |
|---|---|---|---|---|---|---|
| Shelter | Wife | Auntie | Sibling | Boyfriend | | |

Any Children (circle yes or no)

| | | Yes | No | If yes, how many | |
|---|---|---|---|---|---|
| How many Baby Mama's or Deadbeat Daddy's? | | If more than one, please name below. Use separate sheet of paper if more room needed. | | | |
| 1. | | | | | |
| 2. | | | | | |
| 3. | | | | | |

| Ever been married (circle ) | Yes | No | If yes, how many times? | |
|---|---|---|---|---|
| Are you or have you ever been on the Down Low? (circle one) | Yes | No | *(If you answer "Yes"* **STOP RIGHT HERE!!)** | |
| Do you owe child support? | Yes | No | Don't Know | |

*If your ex-wife or ex-husband is getting state benefits (childcare, food stamps, etc), then you owe somebody something. Especially tax payers. **Stop here** and go take care of your kids.*

Education:

| Did you graduate from high school? (circle ) | Yes | No | Name of high school (if yes) | | |
|---|---|---|---|---|---|
| Have you received any of the following? (Circle One) | | | GED | | Diploma |

*If you did not complete any of the above, please **Stop here** *and return to school.*

| Any college? (circle one) | Yes | | No | Still Enrolled: | | Yes | No | Graduated |
|---|---|---|---|---|---|---|---|---|
| Have you ever been to jail? (circle one) | Yes | | No | If yes, state reason? (be very specific) | | | | |

Explain in depth below. Include any court judgment or rulings:



| Have you ever been to prison? (circle one) | | Yes | No | | |
|---|---|---|---|---|---|

*If you have answered yes to the above question, please **Stop here** and call your Parole Officer immediately.

| Employed? (circle) | | Yes | No | *If no, please **Stop here**? No need to complete the application. You are automatically eliminated. |
|---|---|---|---|---|

| If yes, where and how long? | | | | |
|---|---|---|---|---|
| Do you have health insurance? | | Yes | No | |
| When did you last visit the dentist? | | | | |
| Have you been to the doctor recently? | | Yes | No | What for? |

List any (all) illnesses. Use separate sheet of paper if needed.

Do you have or have you had any of the following? *(please circle all that may apply)*

| Hepatitis A or B or C | Herpes | Mononucleosis | HIV/AIDS | The Bird Flu | West Nile Virus | Crabs |
|---|---|---|---|---|---|---|
| Chlamydia | Gonorrhea | SARS | Head Lice | Ringworms | Boils | Sex Change |
| Shingles | Meningitis | Measles | Mumps | Ebola | Bunions | Virus |
| A Cold | Something that you can't spell | | | | | |

*If you have circled any of these, **Stop here**, Do NOT turn in your application. See the doctor immediately!

*Covered*

| | | | | | | pills | |
|---|---|---|---|---|---|---|---|
| | | | | | | | |

| Anything under the kitchen sink |
| Marijuana |

*Please use a separate sheet of paper to compile a list of goals and accomplishments.

By signing below, you agree that all of the information given above is true to the best of your knowledge. For my protection, you may be asked to provide the following information upon request: state ID, birth certificate, recent payroll stub, or a recent clean bill of health from a certified physician or practitioner.

Falsifying information may result in termination of this relationship (if applicable), and a severe whooping from my crazy relatives.

Applicant's Signature                                           Date:

Print Name :

AUTHOR UNKNOWN (Source: E-mail)

This application is based on the characteristics of a carnal mind. It can't provide any insight into the person's spiritual mentality. Especially since we all know a carnal mind can't understand spiritual things. We shouldn't allow such material to deter our minds from seeking Godly counsel when it comes to relationships. It's time to move from desiring fleshly qualities into delighting ourselves in the Lord. Once you develop a relationship with Him you will begin seeing things from a spiritual perspective. Until then, you will still be living in the dark.

# Sistah to Sistah

Society would have you believe approving the right mate is that easy! Wrong, it is harder now because we choose to ignore red flags when dating or courting. Yes, red flags. You know that gut feeling that tells you something isn't right? A carnal mind believes it's their gut feeling or intuition. But, believers know it's their spiritual mind trying to direct you. How many times has the Holy Spirit warned you to stop or get out of a relationship, but you ignored the signs and His voice? I know, too many for you to count. Well, you're not alone.

Society would like to dictate how to recognize a good man. But many people won't explain how to recognize a <u>Godly</u> man. This is partly because society still deals with fleshly unrighteous qualities and characteristics. Instead, believers deal with righteous qualities led by the spirit and soul.

Allow me to share some wisdom I received regarding characteristics over the years.

Here are four important characteristics of a Godly man:

- He has a personal relationship with God.
- Willfully accepts his God-given responsibility.
- Makes time for God at church, home and work.
- Understands Gods order of union.

    A. Personal stability

    B. Gender Relationship

    C. Marriage

Your problem is that you're in love with the thought of being in love. You stop looking for Godly characteristics and choose to ignore spiritual wisdom from messengers. You want to believe men complete you instead of compliment you. According to the word, he can't complete you, because woman was created for man, not the other way around.

You get too dreamy eyed and desperate. Unfortunately, you settle or tolerate foolishness from men who are unequally yoked with you from the *first* conversation or date. You become emotionally attached after a simple text message. You picture him being your husband, babies' daddy, provider, caregiver, maintenance man or midnight hook-up. All of which are unrighteous actions on your part.

You see the red flags, but proceed anyway. Stop becoming attached to men that are <u>recent</u>ly divorced, <u>recent</u>ly dissolved from a relationship or separated from their wife. As you know, <u>recent</u>ly divorced and dissolved situations still have baggage attached. They need time to heal and complete the closure process.

Red Flag: Separated men living apart from their **wife.** Let me stress WIFE! This means, they are not divorced. She still has legal papers on him and vice versa. He's OFF LIMITS no matter what he says. There's nothing Christ-like about dating a married or separated man. Be especially careful when they say, "We have been separated for X years, let me take you to dinner." Realistically speaking, <u>X</u> **years** is more than enough time to get a divorce instead of <u>talking</u> about getting a divorce. Stop entertaining foolishness!

Fleshly men, on the other hand, are the opposite. Some don't care if they are equally yoked with you. They're visual and concerned about what they see or what you can bring to the table. Do you see how short their paragraph is? That is because women are more complicated. But, right when either person starts to feel threatened … oh, let the games begin.

*Covered*

# Games We Play

Ladies, allow me to do an analysis. Dating is like playing checkers and can become time consuming. And we all know checkers is a game a lot of people know how to play, but still lose in the end. They lose because they over anticipate their opponent's next move. The main objective of the game is to remove all your opponent's pieces (your competition, or other women) from the board. You place your checkers on every other square (you mentally space out your, "if he does this… then I will do this," attitude). However, I noticed women and men play games differently. Here's how some women play the game: Let's assume the game is being played at your house. Step 1. Set up the board (your dating atmosphere). From the time you agree to meet, your mind shifts into overdrive with "What If's" and "I need to do's". In a quick moment, you already place one checker on the 'what to wear' square, one checker on the 'what to serve' square, one checker on the 'what music to play' square and one checker on the 'what to drink' square. This is just the beginning, because you have two more rows of anticipated moves. Comically, you can't proceed with any more moves until your date arrives to play the game. Let's just say your date arrives 'on time' to play the game. Step 2. Both of you take turns moving from one space (conversation) to another, all night long. You discuss simple things (diagonal move) then gradually elevate the conversation (another diagonal move) to more thought provoking subject matter (another diagonal move). Usually, by now someone is starting to feel a little uncomfortable with the last subject (another diagonal move) and both are parched. You need time to rethink your strategy with your new opponent. You noticed the move you made with a prior opponent isn't working with your new opponent. Now what do you do? You cannot call your girlfriend and ask for advice. You can't search online for "Dating Mishaps or Do's and Don'ts in Dating". Most assuredly, you can't start the night over and create another board (dating atmosphere). Step 3. It is time for you to try and jump over your date's last subject and re-gain control of the game.

You ponder over the next move because it could be your last. You don't want that to happen because you have not fully survived the aftermath from the last topic. Most of the time, the last subject (final diagonal move) has to do with intimacy. Let's be honest, unless you are naïve, you know exactly what you are doing when you create an alluring atmosphere. Most women want things to happen on their terms of course. You set up the board and diagonal moves to determine how he feels about you prior to your last move, the crowning of the king. (i.e. intimacy). You allow your mind to be manipulated into thinking that crowning the king will remove your competition (another woman) from joining the game. I'm sorry to say, you are sadly mistaken. There have been times when crowning the king only eliminates YOU from the competition, not your opponent. Unfortunately, you got too involved, too serious and moved too fast. Obviously, you forgot it's only a game, I mean date, and not an audition for marriage!

Auditioning on your back or knees for a man is a harlot characteristic! Most importantly, you can't see or hear straight lying on your back. That move distorts your vision of the situation, because a soul tie is being formed in a fluid release.

*Richard's Bible Dictionary* states that a harlot (Heb. 'zonah') is a woman who exchanges sex for money. Well, your date paying for dinner can be considered a payment. Your date purchase of shoes, purses, hair-do's, pedicures, manicures, gas, groceries, theatre tickets, and clothing can be considered payment. He doesn't have to physically put the money in your hand for you to crown him.

However, crowning of the king (intercourse) cheapens you as a woman, even if no money is exchanged. You may not be selling your body for money, but you are selling your soul to the devil. In either case, your moves (sin) grieve the Holy Spirit.

Men, you're not left out of this analysis. The main difference between the way you play is simple. You sit and observe the best way to make fewer moves and get crowned. Again, in either case your moves (sin) grieve the Holy Spirit.

I know you heard the cliché "Don't hate the player, hate the game". Yes, the cliché is used by carnal minds. But it also reiterates that you should be tired of playing games at this stage in your life. Brethren, take the word PLAY out of your vocabulary: Stop playing games; stop playing with peoples' emotions; stop playing house; stop playing momma/daddy to kids that aren't yours and stop playing desperate and needy.

I tried not to say this, but we all know the truth shall *make* you free. I anticipate a mood change with my next statement.

Stop asking your friends to hook you up on blind dates. Stop using your body to allure, entice and sometimes trap each other. Stop allowing sexual tendencies to govern your thoughts and actions. Stop putting yourself in compromising situations that tempt you and your date. Stop allowing thoughts of matrimony to consume your daily routine. You are aware that God gives some *the gift of marriage and others he gives the gift of singleness,* 1 Corinthians 7:7b. Both are a gift from God. Neither is a greater gift than the other. Stop playing the mind, body and soul game with each other. Stop using your body to manipulate your dating situation. You're not Samson and Delilah. Judges 16. You're brothers and sisters in Christ.

I believe this is another reason why Paul addressed this issue to the church in Corinth saying *it is good for man not to touch a woman,* 1 Corinthians 7:1. Ladies, all it takes is one touch from a man, while your flesh is weak, to lead to a lot of immoral fleshly acts. *But every man is tempted, when he is drawn away of his own \*lust (\*desires), and enticed. Then, when lust hath conceived, it bringeth forth sin; and sin, when it is finished, bringeth forth death,* James 1: 14-15 (KJV).

So, pay close attention to what you're observing. Your observation will allow you to sense unrighteousness. Utilize your five senses to oppose unrighteous behavior that tempts you into being drawn away from your own righteous desires.

A big part of lust is to <u>overwhelm</u> you. Another part is to <u>intensify</u> your sexual desire or <u>appetite</u>. Look at the three words underlined. All three have to do with power. And when you relinquish your power and control, you become open to sin being conceived.

We all know there are consequences for your actions. But, rejoice in knowing, *no temptation has overtaken you except such as is common to man. But, God is faithful, and will not allow you to be tempted beyond what you are able; but, with the temptation will also make the way of escape, that you may be able to bear it.* 1 Corinthians 10: 13.

*Your body is the temple of the Holy Spirit,* 1 Corinthians 6:19. He lives in you. If you have been reading your bible, you know that the Trinity consists of The Father, Son, and Holy Spirit. The trinity is the doctrine held by most Christians that there are three divine beings (Father, Son, and Holy Spirit) united in the *one* Supreme Divine Being. So, every time you fornicate YOU, YOUR FORNICATOR AND THE HOLY SPIRIT ARE IN BED TOGETHER! Just the thought of that is NASTY!

Carnal minds call that a three-some or a ménage´ a trois. So, let me paint this picture. I hate to get graphic, but this is how I stopped fornicating.

Question: In the middle of your ménage´ a trios...what would you do if you knew the Holy Spirit was sitting on the edge of the bed watching you? What would go through your mind as the whips and chains are hanging off the bed and He's still watching? What would run through your mind as edible oil is being rubbed on you? Now, He's standing beside the bed looking straight into your eyes? What expression would be on your face? I believe a real woman would be totally embarrassed, ashamed, and feel like a whore/harlot. I believe a man would feel mentally raped, violated, and pimped by the virtues of the woman.

Most importantly, your fornicator knows the ménage´ a trios is *perverted*. Let me remind you of what 'perverted' means: (1) To lead astray morally. (2) To turn to an improper use. (3) To misinterpret, especially deliberately; distort. (4) A person who practices a sexual *perversion*. And 'perversion' means: (1) The act of perverting or state of being perverted; (2) Any of various sexual practices that are regarded as **abnormal.** Random House Webster's Dictionary.

I discovered through my research, seven categories of Mosaic Law. Criminal Law was the third category. Of which fornication, adultery, and homosexuality fell under the sub-category of sexual *crimes*. So, how many crimes have *you* committed while making the Holy Spirit watch? How many crimes have you committed while making the Holy Spirit an accessory?

The Old Testament term for fornication (Heb. 'zanah') (Gk 'porneia, also the root for porno) is often translated as "prostitution." We all know a prostitute (Heb. 'zonah') is a *person* who exchanges sex for money. Men aren't exempt from this grievous sin. *"Do you not know that those who do wrong will have no share in the Kingdom of God? Don't fool yourselves. Those who indulge in sexual sin, who are idol worshipers, adulterers, **male prostitutes**, homosexuals, thieves, greedy people, drunkards, abusers, and swindlers — none of these will have a share in the Kingdom of God."* 1 Corinthians 6: 9-10 (NLT). Whether you call yourself a fornicator, harlot, or prostitute they mean the same thing. Either way, you are selling soul to the devil!

*Covered*

In the Old Testament, a sex crime was a sin against God. It also offended an individual or community. What if you had to compensate an individual every time you offended them by committing a sex crime like fornication or adultery? Again, I believe you would stop your criminal behavior.

The teachers of religious law and Pharisees brought a woman caught in the very act of adultery before Jesus in John 8: 1-11. I'm glad Jesus stooped to the ground, providing a connection with *humility*. Don't be mistaken, people will try to *humiliate* you in order to direct attention from their own unrighteousness. God does today what Jesus did on that day. He redirects the attention back to humanity. Jesus accomplished this when he created a connection to the situation by writing in the dust while listening attentively. Don't think God isn't listening to you or your accusers regarding your situation. In verse 7 Jesus raised himself up and said to them, *"All right, stone her. He who is without sin among you, let him throw a stone at her first."* Their sin may not have been adultery, but they had committed some type of sin, just like this woman. Believers today are repeating the same action by throwing stones and hiding their head. An accuser is no match for Jesus. That is why He reminds us daily that we all have sinned and come short of his glory… but go and sin no more.

One reason you should stop fornicating is that God intended for sexual intercourse to be between a husband and HIS lawful wife. He honors the covenant of marriage, but not sex outside of marriage. 1 Corinthians 6 states the unrighteous will not inherit the kingdom of God. Don't be deceived. Neither fornicators, nor idolaters, nor adulterers, nor homosexuals…

will inherit the kingdom of God. As a fornicator, I saw myself in that scripture. Wow! What an eye-opener.

Rejoice in knowing that God provides a way of escape in verse 11a when he states; "and such WERE some of you." If you confess, repent and turn from the wickedness (See 1 Corinthians 6:11b) you enter another category of being washed, sanctified and justified as a believer in the name of the Lord Jesus Christ and by the Spirit of our God.

It is God's desire that all mankind be saved. He sent His son, Jesus, to die on the cross that we might have life and have it more abundantly. Jesus died a humiliating death in order to redeem us and lead us back to God.

Leading up to the execution, He was scourged, stripped of His clothing, a crown of long twisted thorns was pressed on His head; they spit on Him, they beat Him on the head with a stick, they beat Him with a leather whip containing shreds of metal or bone that *tore* the flesh and later forced him to carry His crossbar to His own barbaric execution. He went through all that pain to *purchase* us for a price. Now, my question to you is, "Are you ready to stop letting sexual immorality be your God?"

# Man Up!

Single/unmarried GENTLEmen, may I have a word with you? I'm so tired of hearing you say a good woman is hard to find. She's not hard to find at all. Most of the time, you're searching for the wrong qualities in a woman, since you're so visual. You tend to think she has to have long hair, pretty eyes and be shapely.

Let me ask you something. How many hair-dos, pedicures, massages, shoes, purses or clothes have you bought with your bill money? How many 'don't leave me', 'kiss-up', 'I'm sorry' or 'please forgive me' gifts have you purchased in order to keep your "arm candy"?

Well, these are vain regrets because they only deal with outer appearance. And unfortunately, weeks or months into a rocky relationship, you regret making those purchases. You want to know why? I hate to say this, but you may still be operating in the flesh, in order to buy her, I mean "impress" her.

And if you are straddling the fence spiritually, you may buy her, I mean "impress" her, with your tithes and offerings. I know, I know, that hurt. But I'm trying to express the importance of understanding that any size woman can be a good find, not just a specific look of a woman. It's what's IN a woman that counts. So, prepare your mind to discern virtuous characteristics from the first conversation.

Now, can I speak to you from my heart? I want to briefly address a few things from a Woman of God's perspective. Keep in mind, most of the issues I addressed with women also apply to you, just change the gender reference. Since men are visual beings, I addressed attire and questionable motives with my Sisters in Christ. In the same respect, women are emotional beings, so I want to specifically address emotions and your visual arm of understanding in dealing with them.

Just like children are a gift from God, women are a treasure from God. We are a treasure chest full of surprises. We need to be appraised properly for you to know how to value our worth. But, to truly understand us you must envision our past infirmities staring you right in the face. We look for your protection in safeguarding our emotions with righteous conversation.

We seek your understanding when issues are revealed from our treasure chest. We desire a sense of security from your arms of comfort. This is achieved by sharing the word of God. It aids us in maturing our spiritual growth. It sets boundaries and limits any premature interactions or unrighteous thoughts.

You're the initiator when engaging in matters of the heart. God has given you the ability to be sensitive to the gift He created from man's rib. He trusts you, as your integrity speaks volumes. Therefore, He expects His image to resonate from your soul when handling His gift. Please keep in mind we are precious jewels and our worth is far above rubies, Proverbs 31: 10-31. And the ruby is considered one of four precious stones. The key word is 'precious.' We all know that anything precious should be handled with respect and care. So, take a stand today. Consult the word in developing righteous healthy relationships that glorify God.

Remember the next generation is watching and waiting to follow your lead. Keep in mind, the woman you may mistreat is someone's mother, sister, daughter or aunt. Or, think about another man mistreating your mother, sister, daughter or aunt. Bottom line, would you want someone to mistreat or take advantage of your female family member? I hope your answer is no! I hope you have enough God in you to want them to be respected. In return, the same respect you want another man to have toward your daughter or mother should be the respect you give to another woman.

You don't want anyone taking advantage of them, you don't want anyone beating on them, you don't want anyone stealing from them, and you don't want anyone mistreating their kids or anything of that nature. And you shouldn't do any of those things to another woman. I know you think I'm describing a worldly person. But no, I am describing believers. You would be surprised at the things going on behind Christian doors. But, I know God is able to do exceedingly and abundantly above anything anyone can ask. So, I am asking Him to birth from you the fruit of the Spirit when dealing with my Sisters.

In case you forgot, the fruit of the Spirit are love, joy, peace, longsuffering, kindness, goodness, faithfulness, gentleness and self-control, Galatians 5:22 (NKJV). I know if you pass this fruit on to your son, he will pass it on to the next generation. Remember, he carries on your seed in name. We must get back to the basics in loving and treating others right. I believe it *begins* with you, but it won't end with you.

The cycle can continue into the next generation of men if you catch hold of a young man today. Teach them that sagging ain't happening. Yes, I said "ain't". Teach them boxers are UNDERwear, not OUTER wear. They were made to go underneath your clothing. The key word is "under," which means not seen or into a position below or beneath something. Webster's Dictionary.

Teach them that there's no amount of money they can pimp a woman for, because Jesus paid it all and all to HIM we owe. Teach them that male harlots (male prostitutes) tickle women with their tongue rings on demand. Teach them that undercover Christian freaks tip out of church for secret rendezvous'.

Teach him how to treat a young lady. Enroll him in a class to develop or nurture his mind, body and soul. Make sure he attends church to feed his spirit. Assist him in reading and understanding the word of God (his sword). Take him around some ole folks to impart wisdom within him. Allow him to show love and kindness by doing for others (washing someone's feet) while volunteering.

Now, regarding self-control, it is time to stop playing the blame game about what your parents didn't do or teach you. It is time to stop corrupting this generation by allowing them to believe it is fine to view pornography. It is time to stop engaging in promiscuous relationships just because your father, grandfather or uncle did it.

It is time to go get your wives, sisters or daughters who are dancing on poles or stripping in clubs. Don't be silent after discovering erotic items in your home. Don't look the other way after finding porn or XXX tapes in your house. Check your phone bill for 1-800 numbers. It's time for you to GET YOUR HOUSE IN ORDER and TAKE BACK CONTROL! In order for this to be done, *"you"* **must first be in order yourself.**

It's time for you to MAN UP and take a stand against the wiles (trick) of the devil. Be the leader (head) God called you to be. Help make a difference today. It is never too late!

# 12

# Relationship Wisdom

## Realistic Tips For Dating

1. **REMAIN CELIBATE!**
   Under NO circumstance should you become intimate or engage in sexual intercourse. Your body is the temple for the Holy Spirit. Don't allow those spirits to enter your temple. Don't disappoint God by choosing intimacy over him. He's worth more than that 5-10 minute thrill.

2. **Masturbation (self gratification) isn't an option.** No, the bible does not specifically say do not masturbate. However, I do know sin begins with a thought (seed). The simple thought of self gratification plants a seed in your mind. We all know seeds grow when you water them. The impure thought of masturbation waters that seed. The more you think about it, the more it grows, until it turns

in a temptation to fornicate or engage into another act of sexual immorality. You dishonor God when you engage in anything that pleases the flesh.

Masturbation falls into that category because it's a fleshly act. And, any fleshly act is sinful. You know your mind has to drift into a <u>demonic illusion</u> or <u>fictitious pleasure</u>, guided by an inanimate (<u>lifeless</u>) object, or your hand. Consider this, there's nothing Godly in the words I just used.

So, throw your vibrators and other sex toys away and give your hand a rest. Every jerk of your wrist, bend of your finger or gyrate of your body, breaks your fellowship with God because your mind has drifted into an impure fleshly thought.

It is written in 1 Corinthians 10: 13, no temptation has overtaken you except such as is common to man; but God is faithful, and will not allow you to be tempted beyond what you are able. But, with the temptation, God will also make the way of escape, that you may be able to bear it. This is obtained by surrendering your thoughts to the Holy Spirit. Allow Him to save your mind by redirecting your thoughts back to God's word.

He wants you to *"meditate on whatever things are true, whatever things are noble, whatever things are just, whatever things are pure, whatever things are lovely, whatever things are of good report, if there is any virtue and if there is anything praiseworthy, meditate on these things. "* Philippians 4:8 (NKJV).

I'm a witness that temptation will leave you after repeating this scripture over and over out loud. The power from the scripture makes the enemy flee and leave you alone.

3. **Get an accountability partner.** Anytime you start feeling tempted, call them to pray with you or provide a mobile rescue, to remove you from the tempting atmosphere. Even if you're on a date or the person is at your house.

4. **Don't turn mingling into cohabitating (shacking/ living together).** It innocently begins when both seem to hit it off and begin dating. One date turns into another date. After which, they seem to be at your home more than at their home. Then they bring articles of clothing over to keep from returning home. Then they bring other items that assist them in getting ready for a date. Before you know it, they have clothes in your closet and you have items at their house. Now, both of you have laid a foundation for shacking and possible fornication. Both of which dishonors God.

5. **Engage in holistic activities** which elevate your spiritual knowledge and contain substance.

6. **Don't irritate her/him** with fussing, nagging or complaints.

7.  **Give each other space** to breathe. You can suffocate each other when you cut of the air flow. You feel like your personal space is being intruded.

8.  **Don't become clingy by trying to fit into their lifestyle.** Remember, you're just dating; you're not married. Each person MUST have a separate life and residence at all times. You can't live in the shadow of another person's life. I feel more women tend to do this than men. More so because we want to prove to the man that we can adapt to their lifestyle, or we will do whatever is necessary to get them. Unfortunately, a person can become clingy and invade the other's personal space to the point where they can't breathe. Allow space for the other person to miss you! If you are around each other all the time, there is nothing to miss and nothing to anticipate.

9.  **Trust each other or stop dating.**

    If there isn't trust, there's no real relationship. Your situation becomes an existence or a figment of your imagination. Both of which, aren't healthy.

10. **Keep your dates fresh, creative and spontaneous, not boring.** Attend Christian events: --revivals, seminars, conferences, concerts and musicals. It won't hurt to even have an extended bible study together.

11. **Don't become a user or an enable, and try not to seem needy.**

Stop paying bills, buying clothes and babysitting kids that aren't yours. If you are single, you're not married. So, stop acting like you are married by commingling most of your personal assets, especially your children. Just like you get emotionally attached to people, your children do too. Then, if the relationship becomes severed, there is a chance your children will feel abandoned.

12. **Don't show lack of confidence, low self-esteem or appear insecure.** You must first love yourself. So, take time to find yourself while working in a ministry for the homeless, nursing homes or the sick and shut-in, helping-hands ministry. There are plenty of ministries that need volunteers. Remember, it isn't about you; it's about glorifying God.

13. **Agree to disagree on subjects without anger.** Dating is supposed to be peaceful, playful and delightful. When the enemy, "anger," enters a relationship, it robs you of the unspeakable joy left in your temple.

14. **Set some standards, limits and remember your moral values.** Return to God's wisdom in His word. It's your foundation. Your parents, grandparents, senior saints and ministry leaders can help in this area because they imparted some values in you. Don't let pride keep you from seeking answers to questions you don't know.

# You're in love with the wrong person when...

- God confirms you're unequally yoked.
- Relationship becomes controlling or abusive.
- Evidence of cheating becomes apparent.
- Little or no compatibility exists.
- Lack of trust becomes apparent.
- You start following them around town.
- You become an interrogator.
- You mistaken love for lust.
- Little or no communication takes place on a regular basis.

# *After you leave a relationship...*

- **Don't date too soon.** Take a 4-6 month *Dating Sabbatical* (break from dating). Stop being in denial and prideful by thinking you're ready to move into another relationship. Use the time to correctly close the prior relationship chapter in your life. Allow your heart to process all of the emotions that come over you. Be still and allow God to purge the residue left lingering in your heart.

  You will cry, pout, laugh and even become angry. Just remember you have to <u>go through</u> a healing process of closure. Don't ignore the emotions that come over you. You must address them with prayer. Quickly moving into another relationship after a break-up is always a train wreck waiting to happen. You must unload the baggage from each relationship before communication can exist in another one. This is a part of the healing process.

- **Don't date on the rebound.** It doesn't fill a void. Only God can fill that void!

*Covered*

- **Allow plenty of healing time.** (Your healing is over when you can discuss that relationship without anger or resentment.)

- **Take time to rediscover yourself.** Spend time getting to know *you*.

- **Do activities with friends and family.** (Don't hibernate in the house, avoid calls or stop attending church). That's when the enemy tries to creep into your mind with a depression lie. Rebuke that lie and live again.

- **Ladies,** if you haven't fully healed, don't give out your phone number to perspective daters. (You may be in denial, but this is still rebounding).

- **Gentlemen,** if you haven't fully healed, don't flirt at meet and greets or Christian events. Men have emotions like women and need to heal. And, it is hard to heal while being comforted by another woman. That's not healing, that's playing games.

- **Separate yourself from situations** that remind you of the past relationship.

- **Get deeper** in the word of God.

- **Increase your commitment** to kingdom work in ministries.

- **DON'T BECOME A RECLUSE.** There's nothing wrong with enjoying social events by yourself! You don't need to always be with groups of people to enjoy life. Utilize this time and remember how to live again. Remember, an idle mind is the devil's workshop. DON'T LET THE ENEMY STEAL YOUR JOY by planting crazy thoughts in your head that can lead to suicidal or other thoughts.

- **Find a new hobby, exercise, volunteer or pamper yourself.** Get your life back; don't let your life get back at you. Remember, you are more than a conqueror.

Lets' move to a touchy subject …

# 13

# A Hot Mess!

**Seasoned saints**…back in the day, mothers would tell you to 'take a bath before bed' and 'change your sheets after three days'. But today, brethren and child/children are both going to bed, laying with filthy people, on dirty sheets, and bringing that spirit into God's house and giving him tainted praise. We all know how a person smells when they try to cover funk with perfume.

Come on now, remember when you left the club Saturday night and woke from your drunken sleep? Your body reeked from the smell of alcohol, smoke, sweat, and maybe some intimate juices too. You wouldn't have time to shower for church, so you would get up and try to conceal Saturday night's evidence with Sunday morning cologne or perfume. We used to call that 'unky', not funky, but today it is called **A HOT MESS!**

There is something wrong with our society when you can lay on dirty sheets, then drape those same sheets around you like a holy robe and wear it to church. What's going on?

Juanita Bynum said, *No More Sheets*. My pastor, Jeffery D. Thomas Sr. said, *Kick the Sheets Back*. I say, how about, *No More Christian Freaks*.

We are freaking at home, school and around our kids. Men are defiling their sons, sons are defiling young children, children are defiling their parents, mothers are defiling their daughters, uncles are defiling their nieces, fathers are defiling their daughters, and aunts are defiling their nephews. The cycle will continue if the stronghold or generational curse is not broken. Society used to imply that other races were committing most of these ungodly acts. Now, family secrets confirm that multiple races are committing many of the same ungodly acts. However, it wasn't spoken about openly. To add insult to injury – all that MESS has funneled into the church and taken a seat on the front row, where the deacons and trustees usually sit.

Undercover Christians or youth used to sit in the back to fool around. Today, filth walks in, passes the back seat, and speaks to his/her "clique" on the way to the front row. They sing, *Hello my name is Victory,* shout all over the church, and after the benediction, put their filthy robe back on. They return home the same way they arrived. Now that's *A Hot Mess*. When are you going to stop playing church? You should know by now, you destroy your witness when the babes in Christ accept the call to discipleship and you're still straddling the fence.

Can you understand when Jesus returned to Jerusalem, entered the temple and began to drive out the merchants and their customers in Mark 11:15? See, you read it, but you didn't think the scripture applied to you. Why, because you're a New Breed Christian from the millennium church. You replaced the merchant table with sexual and immoral acts IN the church. The new age money changer is now pimping your kids, singing in the choir. You moved shacking from your residence to _____ (fill in your church address). Then you have the audacity to change your unlisted number to _____ (fill in your church phone number). This implies that you will not be moving any time soon.

I declare, the devil is a liar because Mark 11:16, (NKJ) states…"and he (Jesus) wouldn't allow anyone to carry wares (particular kind of merchandise) through the temple." The New Living translation states…"he stopped everyone from bringing in merchandise." So, whatever you are selling, pimping or hiding behind, will no longer be bought, sold or exchanged in HIS HOUSE. Mark 11:17 states, "He (Jesus) taught them; His temple will be called the house of prayer for all nations." Well, that means YOUR church! How many people do you think your church will help if they come to worship in an imitation Sodom and Gomorrah atmosphere?

I must remind New Breed Israel of Hosea 2. Don't regain a crown as old Israel (promiscuous woman) and be held to account for the things you have done. You will no longer be God's wife and He no longer your husband. He told you to take off her garish make-up and suggestive clothing and to stop playing the prostitute.

If you don't, He will strip you naked as you were on the day you were born. He will leave you to die of thirst, as in a desert, a dry and barren wilderness. He will not love her children as He would my own because they are not His children! They were conceived in adultery. For their mother (New Breed Israel) is a shameless prostitute and became pregnant in a shameful way. You said, I will run after other lovers and sell myself to them for food, drink clothing. God will strip you naked in public, while all her lovers look on. But, He will win you back!

As a **sentence** for your crime, you will stumble in broad daylight and so will your false prophets. He will destroy you (New Breed Israel). That's why your daughters turn to prostitution, and your daughters-in-law commit adultery. New Breed Israel, you are as stubborn as a heifer. He will put you out to pasture where you will stand alone, unprotected, like a helpless lamb.

Heed the warnings of Hosea or James 1:21 and *"wherefore lay apart all filthiness and superfluity (abundance) of naughtiness, and receive with meekness the engrafted word, which is able to save your souls."* It is time to confess, repent and live a righteous life, pleasing to God.

Women, I know you are tired of defiling the name of Jesus, acting like a nymphomaniac, because I was. So, stop thanking men with carpet burns on your knees while saliva drips from both corners of your mouth. Stop auditioning for men on your backs or knees. Use your back for sleeping and your knees for *praying*.

Men already know fornication is wrong, but they do what we allow them to do. So, hopefully you'll be convicted enough to STOP.

Most importantly, stop using scripture and Sunday morning manna from Heaven to affirm your unsanctioned relationship. The only affirmation you will receive, is conviction from being disobedient. Don't end up in the pits of hell lying on your back.

Must I remind you, *"we are a chosen generation and royal priesthood."* See 1 Peter 2: 9-10. Now, what kind of queen are you if you crown EVERY king that enters your court? Especially, those men that haven't met our Father's seal of approval. Not our earthly father, but our Heavenly Father.

Hypothetically speaking, you're so precious; a man should have to present a dowry to our Heavenly Father in honor of your virtuous qualities. And, if our Father deems him worthy and you're equally yoked, courting/dating may be permitted.

Until then, fill your single time doing the Lord's work. Believe His word and delight yourself in Him and he'll give you the desires of your heart. If you're not single, still believe His word and delight yourself in Him and he'll give you the desires of your heart AS WELL.

My testimony shows you it's time to stop playing church and straddling the fence. It's time to stop hiding behind a church persona or façade. It's time to love God more than sexual immorality, thoughts of dating, thoughts of marriage, or anything else. Your deliverance may not take 30 years of wandering in the wilderness and a 4 year assignment like mine. But, do whatever it takes, you owe God.

Aren't you ready, *yet*?

To God be the glory, Amen!

# <u>WARNING!</u>

If you discover your partner was <u>ever</u> on the down-low (DL) or bi-curious:

- Dry your tears and clean your face.
- Run, don't walk, to the nearest clinic and get a HIV/ AIDS test.
- Or, schedule a doctor's appointment.
- Don't fabricate the purpose for your visit.
- Don't play Russian roulette by delaying testing. You'll put yourself and others at risk!

\*\*\*\*\*\*

To purchase additional copies of this resource:
Covered Ministries, LLC
P.O. Box 6305
Fort Worth, TX, 76115
(817) 905-4581
Include check or money order payment of $13.99 USD
plus $5.00 shipping and handling fee.
Allow 3-4 weeks for delivery.

<u>Order Online:</u> www.Coveredministriesllc.homestead.com

For more information or to schedule speaking engagements, sow seed, or share comments, email:

urepentnow@gmail.com
www.facebook.com/Linda.D.Lee

# WARRIORS

## Round Table & Prayer Warriors

Sis. LaTonya Dacus
Sis. Jacquelin Johnson
Sis. Tonya Williams

\*\*\*\*

## "Labor of Love" Thanks

Chad and Wicks Design
www.wicksdesign.com

I appreciate all of your hard work.
More so, bless you for understanding
the Holy Spirit led changes to the cover.
I will never forget your kindness.

\*\*\*\*

## Special Appreciation

Bridgewater Properties, LLC

Jessica Godbee, Cover Design

Elder Dietrich Pruitt, Logo Design
kingdomkonnectionsdezigns@gmail.com

LaToyin Rollins, Editor
latoyin.rollins@gmail.com

Thank God for leading you to this anointed ministry. Our prayer for you is that the Holy Spirit allow our spiritual senses to minister to you through encouragement and compassion. We believe, with God empowering our steps, total deliverance from sexual immorality is inevitable.

We edify every area of your life through the instructions we receive from the word of God. In doing so, it generates restoration and reconciliation to those that desire to live a righteous life.

## Back 2 Basic Seminar

We commit to repeat, rehearse, and expound on scriptures in teaching women and young ladies the basic principles of how to be 'virtuous' as defined in God's word.

The seminar ministers on some subjects addressed in this book. In addition, it serves as a spiritual activist for purity and abstinence.

CPSIA information can be obtained
at www.ICGtesting.com
Printed in the USA
LVHW021125210720
661193LV00017B/1234